vCenter Troubleshooting

Resolve some of the most commonly faced vCenter problems with the use of this troubleshooting guide

Chuck Mills

BIRMINGHAM - MUMBAI

vCenter Troubleshooting

First published: April 2015

Production reference: 1240415

Published by Packt Publishing Ltd.
Livery Place
35 Livery Street
Birmingham B3 2PB, UK.

ISBN 978-1-78355-403-4

www.packtpub.com

Credits

Author
Chuck Mills

Reviewers
Kenneth van Ditmarsch
Daniel Langenhan

Commissioning Editor
Kunal Parikh

Acquisition Editor
Harsha Bharwani

Content Development Editor
Gaurav Sharma

Technical Editor
Chinmay S. Puranik

Copy Editors
Shambhavi Pai
Trishla Singh
Laxmi Subramanian

Project Coordinator
Harshal Ved

Proofreaders
Safis Editing
Paul Hindle

Indexer
Tejal Daruwale Soni

Production Coordinator
Alwin Roy

Cover Work
Alwin Roy

About the Author

Chuck Mills (@vchuckmills) has been involved in virtualization technologies for more than 12 years and has focused on using those technologies to create efficient and resilient solutions for datacenters and desktops. Chuck is currently the senior technologist for Racktop Systems, Inc. in Fulton, Maryland. Prior to joining Racktop, he was the EUC practice director for GANTECH, Inc. In his previous roles, Chuck led the efforts to create multiple datacenters that were 100 percent virtualized. He coauthored *VMware Horizon 6 Desktop Virtualization Solutions* and has given numerous presentations regarding the benefits of virtualization, including VMworld and VMware Partner Exchange. He is a former member of the VMware Customer Council (VCC), and coleader of the Maryland VMUG, and he has been a vExpert since 2011. Chuck also maintains a blog at www.vchuck.com that is dedicated to virtualization.

I would like to thank my wonderful wife, Michelle, and my children, Bradley, Brooke, Corbin, and Chuck III, for all the support and encouragement they gave me to make this book possible.

I would also like to thank Jonathan Halstuch and Eric Bednash of Racktop Systems for their support and for giving me the opportunity to live my virtualization passion. Thank you Packt Publishing for giving me the opportunity to be a part of this book. Special thanks to the VMware friends I have met over the years. Thank you John Dodge for all your wisdom and Daniel Beveridge for sharing your extensive knowledge. Finally, thank you Dan Berkowitz for continuing to push me forward.

About the Reviewers

Kenneth van Ditmarsch is a very experienced freelance virtualization consultant. As one of the few VMware Certified Design eXperts (VCDX), he offers clear added value in virtualization infrastructure projects. He gained knowledge and extensive project experience especially during his last years at VMware and through several specialized consulting engagements he worked on.

Kenneth agreed to review this book based on his extensive VMware product experience. Also, read Kenneth's personal blog at http://www.virtualkenneth.com around virtualization.

Daniel Langenhan is a virtualization expert with formidable skills in architecture, design, and implementation for large multi-tier systems. His experience and knowledge of process management, enterprise-level storage, and Linux and Windows operating systems has made his business a highly sought-after international consultancy in the Asia Pacific and European regions for multinational clientele in the areas of finance, communication, education, and government. Daniel has been working with VMware products since 2002 and directly associated with VMWare since 2008. He has a proven track record of successful integrations of virtualization into different business areas while minimizing cost and maximizing the reliability and effectiveness of the solution for his clients.

Daniel's expertise and practical approach to VMWare has resulted in the publication of *Instant VMware vCloud Starter*, *VMware View Security Essentials*, *VMware vCloud Director Cookbook*, and *VMware vRealize Orchestrator Cookbook*, all by *Packt Publishing*

He has also lent his expertise to many other publishing projects as a technical editor.

www.PacktPub.com

Support files, eBooks, discount offers, and more

For support files and downloads related to your book, please visit www.PacktPub.com.

Did you know that Packt offers eBook versions of every book published, with PDF and ePub files available? You can upgrade to the eBook version at www.PacktPub.com and as a print book customer, you are entitled to a discount on the eBook copy. Get in touch with us at service@packtpub.com for more details.

At www.PacktPub.com, you can also read a collection of free technical articles, sign up for a range of free newsletters and receive exclusive discounts and offers on Packt books and eBooks.

https://www2.packtpub.com/books/subscription/packtlib

Do you need instant solutions to your IT questions? PacktLib is Packt's online digital book library. Here, you can search, access, and read Packt's entire library of books.

Why subscribe?

- Fully searchable across every book published by Packt
- Copy and paste, print, and bookmark content
- On demand and accessible via a web browser

Free access for Packt account holders

If you have an account with Packt at www.PacktPub.com, you can use this to access PacktLib today and view 9 entirely free books. Simply use your login credentials for immediate access.

Instant updates on new Packt books

Get notified! Find out when new books are published by following @PacktEnterprise on Twitter or the *Packt Enterprise* Facebook page.

Table of Contents

Preface

vCenter is the main component of vSphere and also the primary interface that administrators use to set up, manage, and monitor the vSphere environment. It allows the user to dynamically provision new services, balance resources, and automate high availability.

vCenter Troubleshooting will show you how to approach some of the most common problems when vCenter is not working the way it should. It will also help you isolate the problems and then use a troubleshooting method to resolve the problems you are facing. We will cover the troubleshooting of vCenter areas such as SQL Database, single sign-on (SSO), password issues, monitoring, storage and configuration, and operations manager. We will then move onto grouping similar problems into logical sections, where the administrator can find solutions.

What this book covers

Chapter 1, *vCenter Upgrades and Migrations*, provides an understanding of the best practices and the typical steps when upgrading to vCenter 6.0. The chapter also addresses instances where an installation has started with SQL Express as the vCenter database, but there was a desire or need to upgrade to the full version on SQL Server. It shows the SQL Server upgrade steps. When installing the VCSA, there is usually a DCHP service for that installation, but if not, this chapter will show you how to deploy VCSA without a DCHP server. Further, it will also cover the migration process from the Windows-based (C#) vCenter to the VMware vCenter server appliance.

Chapter 2, *Working with the vCenter Database*, helps diagnose and fix connection problems between the vCenter server and the database that is used to keep the vSphere inventory. vCenter uses the database to keep track of all vSphere information and cannot function without it. The chapter will also help the administrator understand how to recover from an improper shutdown as it pertains to the database.

Chapter 3, Setting Access and Permissions, shows you how to reset or unlock the single sign-on password, which is essential to vCenter. This chapter will also cover the permission difference VCOps and vCenter and assist in the translation of permissions from vSphere to vCOps and how they work together. It will cover the relationship between Active Directory (AD) and vCenter and how to solve possible problems when connecting AD and vCenter.

Chapter 4, Monitoring and Performance Considerations, covers topics with operations manager and how it is used to monitor components of vSphere. It will show how Operations Manager can identify I/O-intensive virtual machines in your environment. The chapter will also explore how vCenter uses Java and how to configure it to obtain the best performance. The chapter will help the administrator correct the problem caused by changes made to vCenter that prevents performance information from being displayed.

Chapter 5, Working with Storage, deals with a select number of storage issues. It will show the administrator how to remove a LUN from multiple ESXi hosts. It will also help you troubleshoot and resolve the problem of snapshot files that are locked and cannot be deleted. It will also cover using vCenter operations for troubleshooting storage devices.

Chapter 6, Solving Some Not-so-common vCenter Issues, helps you fix the problem when no objects show up in your vCenter inventory. The chapter will also help resolve the error message VPXD must be stopped to perform this operation in the VCSA. Finally, the chapter will also show the administrator how to remove plugins that are no longer wanted in the vCenter environment.

Chapter 7, Backup and Recovery, helps the administrator plan for the worst. Protecting the vCenter environment is essential to prevent partial data loss, or a complete loss of the vSphere environment. This chapter will show you how to prepare and recover from this administrator's nightmare. It will show not only what to backup, but also the method you can use to perform the backup. Your backups are useless unless you can recover the information from them. It will also provide the guidance needed to perform a successful recovery.

Chapter 8, Additional Support Methods and Tools, shows the administrator how to use the vCenter support assistant to obtain quicker responses when problems are reported. It also provides information and links to some of the free tools used to support the vSphere environment.

Chapter 9, Troubleshooting Methods, puts together a standard workflow to be used to help solve problems that might arise in your environment. Part of finding a resolution is having an approach that helps you discover and isolate the cause of the problem. Using the workflows will also help collect the information needed for you to resolve the problem yourself or submit the problem to a support service.

What you need for this book

The reader should have a basic understanding of the following concepts, which are integral to the implementation and management of vSphere:

- LAN and WAN networking
- Storage
- Server Hardware
- Microsoft Active Directory
- Microsoft Windows Server (2008 and/or 2012)
- VMware vCenter
- VMware vSphere along with basic administration
- VMware vCops (vRealize)

The following software applications are required to implement the solutions described in this book:

- VMware vSphere 5.5 and related products found at https://my.vmware. com/web/vmware/info/slug/datacenter_cloud_infrastructure/ vmware_vsphere/5_5
- VMware vSphere 5.5 documentation found at https://www.vmware.com/ support/pubs/vsphere-esxi-vcenter-server-pubs.html
- Microsoft Windows Server 2008/2012 or installation media
- Putty found at http://www.putty.org/
- WinSCP found at http://winscp.net/eng/download.php

Who this book is for

This book is for vSphere administrators who understand that troubleshooting vCenter can be frustrating and in some cases downright difficult. The vSphere Enterprise infrastructure is made up of complex pieces of both hardware and software. The contents of this book will not only help you isolate the problem you are facing, but will also help you use a troubleshooting workflow to get a resolution. The focus of this book is vCenter, configuration manager, and operations troubleshooting. This book will give you the problem-solving methods to build confidence in dealing with the day-to-day problems an administrator might encounter in the vSphere environment.

Conventions

In this book, you will find a number of styles of text that distinguish between different kinds of information. Here are some examples of these styles, and an explanation of their meaning.

Code words in text, database table names, folder names, filenames, file extensions, pathnames, dummy URLs, user input, and Twitter handles are shown as follows: "Run `regedit` again and move to `HKLM\System\CurrentControlSet\Services\` and remove the old service values from SQL Express from the `DependOnService` Multi string found in the vCenter services."

A block of code is set as follows:

```
com.rsa.db.type=MSSQL.
com.rsa.db.instance=RSA. (your RSA instance dbname is)
com.rsa.db.msserverinstance= . (Leave empty when using the default
    MSSQLSERVER instance on the target server)
com.rsa.db.hostname=destinationSQL server.
com.rsa.db.port=1433.
```

Any command-line input or output is written as follows:

```
vi /etc/sysconfig/networking/devices/ifcfg-eth0
```

New terms and **important words** are shown in bold. Words that you see on the screen, in menus or dialog boxes for example, appear in the text like this: "Navigate to **Start** | **Run**, type `regedit`, and then click on **OK**."

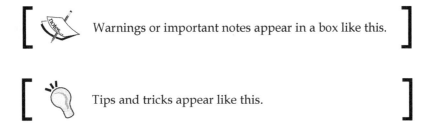

Warnings or important notes appear in a box like this.

Tips and tricks appear like this.

Reader feedback

Feedback from our readers is always welcome. Let us know what you think about this book—what you liked or may have disliked. Reader feedback is important for us to develop titles that you really get the most out of.

To send us general feedback, simply send an e-mail to `feedback@packtpub.com`, and mention the book title via the subject of your message.

If there is a topic that you have expertise in and you are interested in either writing or contributing to a book, see our author guide on `www.packtpub.com/authors`.

Customer support

Now that you are the proud owner of a Packt book, we have a number of things to help you to get the most from your purchase.

Errata

Although we have taken every care to ensure the accuracy of our content, mistakes do happen. If you find a mistake in one of our books—maybe a mistake in the text or the code—we would be grateful if you would report this to us. By doing so, you can save other readers from frustration and help us improve subsequent versions of this book. If you find any errata, please report them by visiting `http://www.packtpub.com/submit-errata`, selecting your book, clicking on the **errata submission form** link, and entering the details of your errata. Once your errata are verified, your submission will be accepted and the errata will be uploaded on our website, or added to any list of existing errata, under the Errata section of that title. Any existing errata can be viewed by selecting your title from `http://www.packtpub.com/support`.

Piracy

Piracy of copyright material on the Internet is an ongoing problem across all media. At Packt, we take the protection of our copyright and licenses very seriously. If you come across any illegal copies of our works, in any form, on the Internet, please provide us with the location address or website name immediately so that we can pursue a remedy.

Please contact us at `copyright@packtpub.com` with a link to the suspected pirated material.

We appreciate your help in protecting our authors, and our ability to bring you valuable content.

Questions

You can contact us at `questions@packtpub.com` if you are having a problem with any aspect of the book, and we will do our best to address it.

1
vCenter Upgrades and Migrations

Upgrades and migrations can be scary at times, and with vCenter at the heart of your Virtual environment, be sure to take time to research, plan, and review the steps for your process. It is also imperative that you fully understand and test the new product before moving it to production. This chapter will provide the following information:

- Upgrading vCenter to vSphere 6
- Migrating vCenter from SQL Express to SQL Server
- Deploy vCenter Server Appliance with no DHCP server
- Upgrading from Windows vCenter 5.1 to vCenter Server Appliance

Best practices for upgrading to vCenter Server

When you migrate to vSphere 6.0, you need to perform all the steps in sequence to avoid frustration, loss of time, and, most importantly, possible data loss. Before you upgrade, you should consider a roll back plan that could include backups and/or snapshots. After you upgrade each component, there is no option to go back. Once you migrate to vCenter Server 6.0, you cannot revert to vCenter Server 5.x without performing your recovery process mentioned earlier.

Good planning and preparation includes research on the following:

- The back up and restoration of vCenter components
- Reading Release Notes for the targeted release
- Researching the Web for others that have performed the upgrade

This will help you in preparing yourself for the update, as it could help you avoid using your recovery plan.

Verifying basic compatibility before upgrading the vCenter Server

You want to verify that all the equipment (hardware) in your environment is going to be compatible with the new software before you perform the upgrade. You should check the *VMware Compatibility Guide*, found at http://www.vmware.com/resources/compatibility.

Verifying your hardware before the upgrade is better than finding out that it's not compatible after the upgrade. Remember to check that plug-ins, such as multi-path IO and any other features you are using will not cause you problems. If you're using products such as Horizon View or Sire Recovery Manager (SRM), make sure you verify the products for any possible conflicts. Also, check any third-party solutions you are using and make sure they can be used with the upgrade you are planning.

Preparing the database before the upgrade

You should verify that the existing database will be supported for the version of vCenter Server you are upgrading to. Reference the *VMware Product Interoperability Matrixes* found at http://www.vmware.com/resources/compatibility/sim/interop_matrix.php.

Perform a full backup of your vCenter Server database, along with the Inventory Service database. Refer to the vendor documentation based on the vCenter Server database type you are using.

To perform backups on the Inventory Service database for Windows, use the information found at https://pubs.vmware.com/vsphere-50/index.jsp?topic=%2Fcom.vmware.vsphere.install.doc_50%2FGUID-518228D1-E305-457C-B552-50DAB4BDF6B1.html.

Also, make sure that permissions are set correctly (DBO) on your vCenter Server database.

Verifying network prerequisites before upgrading

You are going to want to make sure your network is working correctly and that it meets all connectivity requirements for the upgrade of vCenter:

1. Check the **fully qualified domain name** (**FQDN**) of the system on which you will perform the upgrade to make sure it can resolve to the other components.

2. Open the Command Prompt and use nslookup, followed by the hostname of your vCenter (for example, m-vcenter-01). This should return the IP address that is assigned to that system. You should also see the name and IP address of your domain controller. If this is successful, the FQDN should be resolvable.

```
Command Prompt
Microsoft Windows [Version 6.1.7601]
Copyright (c) 2009 Microsoft Corporation.  All rights reserved.

C:\Users\chuck>nslookup m-vcenter-01
Server:  m-dc-01.kingbrook.net
Address:  192.168.1.10

Name:    m-vcenter-01.kingbrook.net
Address:  192.168.1.11
```

3. Now, let's check the DNS reverse lookup and make sure it returns your FQDN name when you use the IP address for the vCenter Server. Do not perform this from the vCenter Server, but from another workstation.

4. If you use DHCP instead of an assigned IP (static) address on the vCenter Server (which is *not* the best practice), check the name to make sure it is correct in **domain name service** (**DNS**). When pinging the name of the vCenter, you should see that the correct IP address is returned. This is shown in the following screenshot:

```
C:\Users\chuck>ping m-vcenter-01

Pinging m-vcenter-01.kingbrook.net [192.168.1.11] with 32 bytes of data:
Reply from 192.168.1.11: bytes=32 time<1ms TTL=128
Reply from 192.168.1.11: bytes=32 time<1ms TTL=128
Reply from 192.168.1.11: bytes=32 time<1ms TTL=128
Reply from 192.168.1.11: bytes=32 time<1ms TTL=128

Ping statistics for 192.168.1.11:
    Packets: Sent = 4, Received = 4, Lost = 0 (0% loss),
Approximate round trip times in milli-seconds:
    Minimum = 0ms, Maximum = 0ms, Average = 0ms
```

5. Let's do the same type of testing with your ESXi host. Again, make sure you can ping both the IP address and the name of the host and get the correct information back. The ping to the vCenter from the host is shown in the following screenshot:

```
192.168.1.40 - PuTTY                                                    _  □  x

login as: root
Using keyboard-interactive authentication.
Password:
The time and date of this login have been sent to the system logs.

VMware offers supported, powerful system administration tools.  Please
see www.vmware.com/go/sysadmintools for details.

The ESXi Shell can be disabled by an administrative user. See the
vSphere Security documentation for more information.
~ # ping m-vcenter-01
PING m-vcenter-01 (192.168.1.11): 56 data bytes
64 bytes from 192.168.1.11: icmp_seq=0 ttl=128 time=0.805 ms
64 bytes from 192.168.1.11: icmp_seq=1 ttl=128 time=0.462 ms
64 bytes from 192.168.1.11: icmp_seq=2 ttl=128 time=0.473 ms

--- m-vcenter-01 ping statistics ---
3 packets transmitted, 3 packets received, 0% packet loss
round-trip min/avg/max = 0.462/0.580/0.805 ms
~ #
```

6. If your identity source is going to be **Active Directory** (**AD**), you want to make sure you have everything configured correctly. Your DNS lookup along with the reverse lookup of your **domain controller** (**DC**) should have the DNS entries for the **Single Sign-On** (**SSO**) Server machines. Try to ping your domain (for example, kingbrook.net), and you should get the IP address of your DC. This is shown in the following screenshot:

```
C:\Users\chuck>ping kingbrook.net

Pinging kingbrook.net [192.168.1.10] with 32 bytes of data:
Reply from 192.168.1.10: bytes=32 time<1ms TTL=128
Reply from 192.168.1.10: bytes=32 time<1ms TTL=128
Reply from 192.168.1.10: bytes=32 time<1ms TTL=128
Reply from 192.168.1.10: bytes=32 time<1ms TTL=128

Ping statistics for 192.168.1.10:
    Packets: Sent = 4, Received = 4, Lost = 0 (0% loss),
Approximate round trip times in milli-seconds:
    Minimum = 0ms, Maximum = 0ms, Average = 0ms

C:\Users\chuck>nslookup m-dc-01
Server:  m-dc-01.kingbrook.net
Address:  192.168.1.10

Name:    m-dc-01.kingbrook.net
Address:  192.168.1.10
```

Verifying whether ODBC communicates with the database

Verify the System DSN settings to make sure that the vCenter Server is configured correctly to communicate with the database.

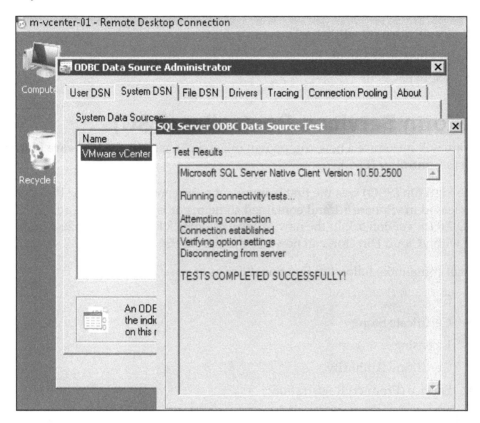

Verifying whether time is synchronized across the vSphere environment

Verify whether your hosts on the current vSphere network have their internal clocks synchronized before you begin the migration of the vCenter Server (Windows or Appliance). If the clocks are unsynchronized, there could be problems with authentication, which could cause your upgrade to fail, or possibly prevent the vpxd service used by VCSA from beginning.

New and updated information in vSphere 6

vSphere 6 contains a few new features and also provides updates to some of the existing features. This section will highlight both the new and updated features found in the vSphere 6 release. The information will be on the following:

- Platform Service Controller
- vCenter Server Appliance
- vSphere Web Client
- vSphere Client

Platform Services Controller (PSC)

VMware will introduce a new component in version 6 named the **VMware Platform Services Controller** (**PSC**).

Single Sign On (**SSO**) was the first component to be converted into the PSC. SSO was released in vSphere 5.1 and contained some major issues. This forced a rebuild to SSO 2.0 for version 5.5. In the new release, vCenter, vRealize, vRealize Automation along with vCloud Director, can now use the shared PSC component.

PSC will contain the following functionalities as of now:

- SSO
- Certificate Store
- Licensing
- Certificate Authority
- Service (Product) Registration

PSC uses the vPostgres database that is integrated into vCenter and the database is the same in both Windows and Appliance versions. PSC also self-replicates; it doesn't use ADAM, which means it is now possible to replicate the Windows vCenter and vCenter appliance between each other.

You can embed PSC within vCenter or use an external database instead of the vPostgres database. The guidance from VMware, if you are running less than eight vCenters, is that it is best to use the embedded PSC, so that vCenter will only connect to the internal PSC.

If you are going to have more than eight vCenters, VMware recommends you use an external PSC, rather than using the embedded one. This way, you can setup PSC in a highly available and load-balanced service sharing between all of your vCenters.

The Certificate Store and the **Certificate Authority (CA)** are new components that will help you with vSphere certificates management. The **VMware Certificate Authority (VMCA)**, which is also new, performs as the root certificate authority and manages its own certificates, or it can handle certificates from an external certificate authority (CA). VMCA allows the provisioning for each ESXi host requiring the signed certificate. This will be added to the vCenter inventory as part of the upgrade. This provides the viewing and managing of the vSphere Web Client certificates, which allows the management of the entire workflow of the certificate lifecycle with the new VMCA.

vCenter Server Appliance

The management limits of **vCenter Server Appliance (VCSA)** have also been expanded. With version 5.5, you could manage up to 100 hosts and up to 3,000 powered on Virtual Machines (VMs). Now, version 6 of vSphere allows you to manage 1,000 hosts and an increase of 10,000 powered on VMs. IBM DB2 continues to be the embedded database, and Oracle remains as the only supported external database. This is because Microsoft will not officially support the ODBC driver for Linux; the driver that is currently used is community supported.

vSphere web client

The web client continues increased performance gains, along with tagging improvements and many other new functions. Flash is still used, which means there is not a native HTML5 web client for now.

vSphere Client

VMware is keeping the VI Client (C#) for at least the next few releases. Progress continues with the web client and there are continuous improvements to the speed. So far, most customer feedback has been a preference for the older, yet familiar, clients. At this point in time, there will be no new functionality added to the old client, but the support will remain. Therefore, the old client will manage less functions than the new VCSA.

Steps for upgrading vCenter

Now that we have completed the overview of the new and updated components, let's begin the steps needed to upgrade vCenter.

Remember to always check the *What's New in VMware vSphere 6.0* document found on the VMware website to find the most current information about the product. The *What's New in VMware vSphere 6.0* can be found at `http://www.vmware.com/files/pdf/vsphere/VMware-vSphere-Whats-New.pdf`.

The new vCenter installer for the Windows version has been streamlined. Now, there is a return to a single installer, with all input collected up front. There is also an improved pre-check function with more items checked. You also have a choice between the external (pre-existing) or the internal (embedded) option of PSCs during the installation process.

The procedure for upgrading has not changed since the last version of vCenter. The following are the vCenter upgrades that you can perform from a standalone installer or Update Manager:

1. vCenter is the first component that is upgraded. If VCSA is used, you might be required to install a new VCSA and then import the information from the previous version.

2. The next component to upgrade is VUM (Windows based vCenter) along with the plugins you are using. Plugins interact with your host and need to be upgraded before the hosts are upgraded.

3. The next step is to upgrade your hosts. Use the newly upgraded VUM and create new baselines with drivers and plugins. Then, upgrade your hosts in a rolling fashion.

4. The next step is to update the Virtual Machines' (VM) tools and virtual hardware.

5. Next, upgrade any vDSes using the following steps:

   Create a backup of your dvSwitch :

   1. Use the web client to log in to the vCenter.

   2. Browse and select the dvSwitch to **Backup**.

   3. Go to **Actions | All vCenter Actions | Export Configuration**.

   4. Select **Distributed Switch and Port Groups.**

   5. Enter the description for the dvSwitch export.

   6. Click on **OK**.

   Then upgrade the dvSwitch:

   1. Use the web client to log in to the vCenter.

   2. Browse and select your dvSwitch to **Upgrade**.

   3. Go to **Action | Upgrade Distributed Switch**.

Review the upgrade version and features available as part of this version:

1. Click on **Next**.
2. Verify the compatibility for the dvSwitch upgrade.
3. Click on **Next**.

Some of the features need additional conversion setup (enhanced LACP support):

1. Select the **Enhance the LACP support** checkbox.
2. Click on **Finish**.

Once the dvSwitch is upgraded, it cannot be downgraded to a previous version and you cannot add older VMware ESX/ESXi servers to the upgraded dvSwitch.

6. Now, upgrade the datastores from VMFS3 to VFMS5 (if upgrading from 5.1 only).
7. Now you can complete other components in your environment such as VDP, vCO, View, vCD, and so on. Remove any snapshots created during the upgrade that are not needed.

Migrating vCenter from SQL Express to SQL Server

While SQL Express is never recommended for a production environment, many times the setup of vCenter is completed with SQL Express for a **Proof of Concept** (**POC**), Pilot or a Test/Development environment. For various reasons, there might be a time you want or need to migrate from SQL Express to the full SQL Server. So, for whatever reason you might have to perform the process, here are the steps used to migrate from SQL Express to the full SQL version:

* Migrate the SSO database (vCenter 5.1 only)
* Migrate the vCenter Database
* Change the vCenter ODBC connection
* Recreate the SQL Jobs

But before you begin, here are a few items to document to make sure the migration goes as smoothly as possible:

* Names of the databases
* Current administration users and the correct passwords

- Target SQL Server Ports
- A decision on the mode of authentication you are going to use

Make sure you check the interoperability of your vCenter with the planned database version and verify that they support each other.

You will need to schedule some downtime of both SSO and your vCenter. While you are moving the database and the services between servers, vCenter and SSO services must be stopped. They will need to be stopped until the data is copied and the configurations are changed. No Virtual Machine workload is touched and it can remain running. If needed, your host can be managed using the standalone vSphere client while the migration is in progress.

Create back-ups of the items that are to be changed such as any files, registry keys, and other items that would need to be recovered if something goes wrong.

Migrating the SSO database

Use this process if you are migrating from a pre-5.5 version. SSO in vCenter 5.5 does not use a database.

If you are not sure of the current password for the RSA_USER/RSA_DBA, you will need to go to the `SSOServer\utils` folder. Open an administrative command prompt and type the following:

```
ssocli manage-secrets -a listallkeys
```

Make sure both vCenter Single Sign-On services are stopped. After verifying that the services are stopped, you can:

- Backup and restore the database files to the target SQL Server
- Copy the database files to the target SQL Server

Two SQL Server users are created when installing SSO:

- RSA_DBA
- RSA_USER

The RSA_DBA is the account used during an installation and is not needed for the migration. During the migration process, the RSA_USER will be used. The login/ user is added to the target SQL Server and the password along with the required permissions are set.

Open an administrative elevated command prompt and move to the default directory of the SSO server `directory\utils`. Type in the following:

```
ssocli configure-riat -a configure-db –database-host newdbhost –
database-port newdatabaseport –rsa-user RSA_USER –rsa-user-password
password -m master_password
```

In the preceding code, replace the following:

- Database hostname
- Database port number `1433` for standard SQL
- RSA_USER password
- `-m` master password for the `Admin@System-Domain` password

The rsa-user password will only work with the rsa-user option.

Prepare to edit two files `jndi.properties` and `config.properties` using your preferred text editor (for example, `Notepad.exe`) and using elevated permissions.

For the first file, `SSOServer\webapps\ims\web-inf\classes\jndi.properties`, check the following values:

```
com.rsa.db.type=MSSQL.
com.rsa.db.instance=RSA. (your RSA instance dbname is)
com.rsa.db.msserverinstance= . (Leave empty when using the default
    MSSQLSERVER instance on the target server)
com.rsa.db.hostname=destinationSQL server.
com.rsa.db.port=1433.
```

Pay special attention to `com.rsa.instanceName` and remember that this does not refer to the SQL Instance. This refers to the SSO instance and you should not change this.

For the second file, `SSOServer\webapps\lookupservice\WEB-INF\classes\config.properties`, check the following values:

```
db.url=jdbc:jtds:sqlserver://;serverName=;portNumber=1433;database
    Name=RSA. PortNumber has to be added here.
db.user=RSA_USER
db.pass=yourpassword
db.type=mssql
db.host=destination SQL server fqdn.
```

Make the changes to the lines in order to match your environment. Now, save the files and start the service for your vCenter Single Sign-On.

Migrating the vCenter database

Stop the vCenter services if they are not already stopped. Include all the services for vCenter, excluding Update Manager, SSO, and Orchestrator. After all the services are stopped:

1. Backup and restore the database files to the target SQL Server.
2. Copy the database files to the target SQL Server.

Then, create the login/user to the target SQL Server, and set the required password and permissions. The user for the vCenter database must be db_owner and also dbo on the Microsoft DB system database can be found on the target server.

Now, use the ODBC Manager (64-bit) to change the System DSN being used by your destination SQL Server.

- When using the default MSSQL Server installation, the MSSQLSERVER instance does not need to be filled, a connection will use the hostname for the SQL server.
- When using Windows credentials (instead of SQL Authentication), the ODBC is changed in the service account user. Modify the default database value to the default name of VIM_VCDB. If you did not change it or if you decided to use a new name for the database, you would type it here.

After the changes are complete, check the connection to verify whether it works.

Changing the vCenter ODBC connection

The next step is to modify the ODBC connection found in the registry:

Navigate to **Start** | **Run**, type regedit, and then click on **OK**. This will start the Registry Editor and the window will open. Move to HKEY_LOCAL_MACHINE | SOFTWARE | VMware, Inc. | VMware VirtualCenter and make a change to the key DbInstanceName by removing its current **Value data**. Do not delete this key. See the following screenshot:

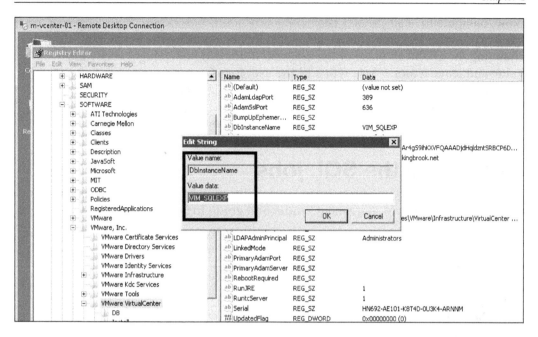

Then change the key `DbServerType`. Edit the **Value data** from SQL Express value `Bundled` to `Custom`, as displayed in the following screenshot:

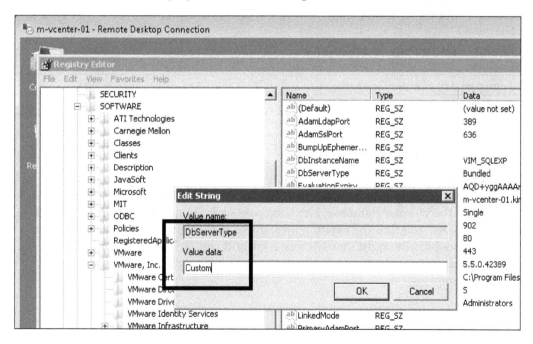

Now, navigate to `HKEY_LOCAL_MACHINE | SOFTWARE | VMware, Inc. | VMware VirtualCenter | DB` and change key 4. Do this by entering the new ODBC driver, changing the ODBC in place of the original. If this did not change, verify the value and leave it alone. You will add the user for vCenter Server SQL to key 2. You need to set the password that is kept in key 3. This is completed by opening an Administrator command prompt and typing `C:\Program Files\VMware\Infrastructure\VirtualCenter Server\vpxd.exe -p`.

Recreating the SQL jobs

Now, on the SQL Server, you need to recreate the SQL jobs. This is completed by using the SQL Server Management Studio and going to SQL Server Agent.

Use the following list to create the job list:

Rollup job	SQL job filename
Event Task Cleanup vCenter Database	`job_cleanup_events_mssql.sql`
Past Day stats rollup vCenter Database	`job_schedule1_mssql.sql`
Past Month stats rollup vCenter Database	`job_schedule3_mssql.sql`
Past Week stats rollup vCenter Database	`job_schedule2_mssql.sql`
Process Performance Data vCenter Database	`job_dbm_performance_data_mssql.sql`
Property Bulletin Daily Update vCenter Database	`job_property_bulletin_mssql.sql`
Topn past day vCenter Database	`job_topn_past_day_mssql.sql`
Topn past month vCenter Database	`job_topn_past_month_mssql.sql`
Topn past week vCenter Database	`job_topn_past_week_mssql.sql`
Topn past year vCenter Database	`job_topn_past_year_mssql.sql`

To add the jobs, browse to `C:\Program Files\VMware\Infrastructure\VirtualCenter Server\sql` and open the equivalent SQL file using `Open | file` and choose the vCenter database. Next, execute each Query and continue through each one. When you find the existing jobs, make sure to check that each matching SQL user in jobs is the right one. Choose a job and right–click on it; then go to properties to make sure the user and database name is right. If they are incorrect, recreate them.

Review the `vcdb.properties` file by going to `C:\ProgramData\VMware\VMware VirtualCenter` (for Windows 2008R2 and higher). Make sure to use Explorer to uncheck hidden and protected files. Then, edit the `vcdb.properties` file value `url= ;integratedSecurity\` to:

- `false` – For SQL authentication
- `true` – For Windows authentication

The following screenshot shows the edited `vcdb.properties` file value `url= ;integratedSecurity\` is set to `true`:

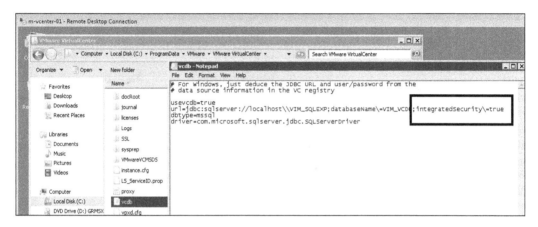

The remaining should match `sqlserver://<your SQL server>\\SQL instance;databaseName=\dbname; dbtype=mssql`.

Check to be sure the Windows user has the permissions to the SQL database. The user also needs to run **VMware VirtualCenter Management Webservices** and **VMware VirtualCenter**. Run `regedit` again and move to `HKLM\System\ CurrentControlSet\Services\` to remove the old service values from SQL Express from the `DependOnService` Multi string found in the vCenter services. Do not delete the value, just remove the VIM_SQLEXP from the data. The other dependencies should not be changed. Start the service for vCenter and use the logs to verify everything has started up.

Deploying vCenter Server Appliance with no DHCP server

When you normally deploy the vCenter Server Appliance, a DHCP server is present and the appliance will get the IP address from it. But what if, for whatever reason, there was no access to a DHCP server for the deployment?

You will need to assign an IP address (static) for your network (VLAN or port group), along with the proper subnet mask. You then need to connect to the host that contains the VCSA appliance using the C# client. Right-click on the VCSA appliance and choose open console. Then, log in to the appliance using the supplied default username of root and vmware as the default password. After logging in, you will be presented with the Linux CLI. Use the following procedure to provide an IP address for your appliance.

Use the following command to change the interface configuration file:

```
vi /etc/sysconfig/networking/devices/ifcfg-eth0
```

From here, you will be using the screen-oriented text edit vi to make changes to the file. If you are familiar with this editor, this should be easy. If not, follow the procedure closely and the changes will be completed without a problem. Inside the vi Editor, use your arrow keys to position yourself in the file. Sometimes, using the arrow keys on the keypad causes problems, so use the non-keypad arrow keys. Now, move to the line that contains BOOTPROTO and press the *E* key, or the right arrow key, to move to the end of the line. By pressing the *I* key, you are now in edit mode and can make modifications to the file. Use the *Backspace* key to delete dhcp and replace it with static.

Continue to use the arrow keys to move to the bottom of the file and insert the following lines:

- TYPE=Ethernet
- USERCONTROL=no
- IPADDR=the IP address you obtained
- NETMASK=the mask you obtained
- BROADCAST=actual IP broadcast address

It should look something like this:

Now, press the *Esc* key, enter a colon (`:`), and type `wq`, and hit the *Enter* key.

You should get a message that shows the `ifcfg-eth0` file was written. Now, restart the network service: `service network restart`.

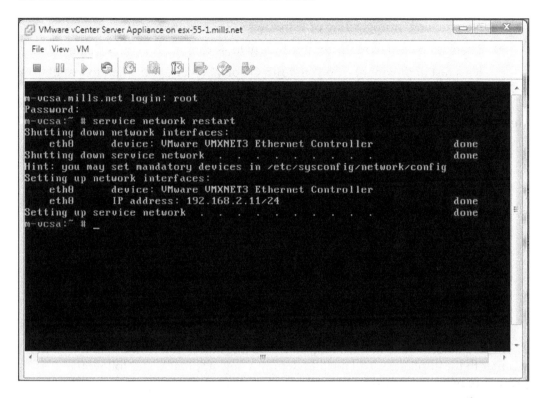

Typing `ifconfig` should show the new IP address you just entered on `eth0`, so verify that you can ping other addresses on the same network.

If you run into problems, double check your IP address, your submask, and the VM port group. Now, with the new IP address, you can get to the VCSA appliance by opening a browser and entering `https://10.10.1.50:5480`.

Upgrading from Windows vCenter 5.1 to vCenter Server Appliance

There is a possibility that VMware will discontinue the Windows vCenter application. You can see it with every new vCenter Release that there is a push towards using the VCSA to manage the vSphere environment. Even now, some newer features in vSphere can't be used from the traditional Windows-based client.

There are several benefits to using VCSA, but there are also some limits.

Here are the benefits of using the VCSA:

- There is no Windows OS license for vCenter Server
- No patching or upgrading of Windows OS is required
- There is no need to maintain third-party tools running on your vCenter Server
- It's a fast deployment—no Windows OS or vCenter application to install
- It's possibly the vCenter of the future

Here are the current limits when using the VCSA:

- Oracle is the only supported external database
- The VCSA is **Software Und System Entwicklung** (**SUSE**) distribution and there are no OS-level patches from VMware
- You would need a certain amount of Linux experience when using the appliance
- No Update Manager
- Problems occur when running local scripts (alarms)
- No integration of Powershell into Alarm execution
- No integration of already existing Windows system monitoring tools

There are no automated tools to help with this migration from Windows vCenter to the appliance. You need to deploy a new appliance and follow the procedure mentioned next to move the host from your original Windows version to the appliance.

Here are a few things to complete before you begin:

- Document the current resource pool configurations
- Document the **High Availability** (**HA**) exception and settings
- Record all DRS rules and groups (you will create the rules after the new vCenter connects to the VMs)
- Document and verify the port configurations of the physical network
- Have Update Manager on the Windows version of vCenter in order to upgrade the host to 5.5 after the migration

After you feel that you have the information you need to make sure you understand your environment, you can schedule some downtime and begin the following migration process:

1. Install, configure, and verify the new production VCSA. Make you can login and then recreate your resource pools, folder structure, and the permissions to match the current environment.

2. If using vSphere Replication, disable it along with HA on the old vCenter.

3. Halt DRS by switching it to manual mode. Your resource pools will be removed if you disable DRS.

4. It is a good idea to export from the old environment and then import the vSphere Distributed Switches (vNDS). This makes the rebuilding process easier, if needed. If you are going from version vSphere 5.1 to VCSA 5.5, keep the current version of the distributed switch. You will upgrade this later after you import the host, which is still at 5.1.

5. Then, remove all additional components from vCenter such as vRealize and other third-party consoles from the old vCenter.

6. Move the VMs to standard virtual switches by using the secondary links for the standard vSwitch. When you add a host to a virtual distributed switch, there you will specify the uplink NIC for hosts and vCenter will assign that NIC to the first uplink slot.

7. Remove the ESXi hosts from the old vDS.

8. Now, disconnect (do not remove), one at a time, each ESXi host from your Windows-based vCenter and add them to the new VCSA. Try to keep the same resource pools using the documentation that was created before the process.

9. Verify that the resource pools are correct and then create DRS & HA rules from the information you gathered before the migration.

10. Add the new imported ESXi hosts to the configured VCSA vDS. Remove the standard vSwitch along with re-adding the NIC to the secondary uplink.

11. Shut down the old vCenter.

12. Re-enable HA and put DRS in fully automated mode on the new vCenter.

13. Move any DNS names related to services.

14. Use Update Manager to update your hosts to 5.5.

15. Migrate your virtual distributed switch to 5.5.

Check and double check along the way to make sure each step is completed to your satisfaction. As with most projects, take the time to verify and document what you have. Put together a plan and always have a procedure to go back to, if needed.

Summary

This chapter has provided an introduction to the troubleshooting solutions you will find in the remaining chapters. It is very important when installing or updating any product to be sure to take the time to fully research the information on the new release or upgrade. Then, plan your process and know the options for recovery before you review your work. Take the time to try to understand how the new product is going to function on the existing equipment before moving it to production.

The next chapter will cover the topic of the vCenter database. vCenter uses the database to keep track of all the vSphere information and cannot function without it. In the next chapter, we will review fixing server services and database issues. The chapter will also help the administrator understand how to recover from an improper shutdown pertaining to the database.

2
Working with the vCenter Database

This chapter will focus on the vCenter database. The last chapter showed you how to move from SQLExpress to the Full SQL Server. Now, let's review some common questions regarding items such as knowing the location of your database, troubleshooting growth, and other issues that keep an administrator up at night.

The vCenter Server uses a database for the storage and organization of information for the server. Each instance of vCenter Server needs to have its own dedicated database.

 As a note, VMware announced the end of availability of vCenter Server Heartbeat. Support for the product will end in September 2018. Administrators should leverage features such as vSphere High Availability along with other best practices to deploy vCenter Server with a management cluster.

The schema cannot be shared between instances of vCenter Server, although multiple databases of vCenter are allowed to exist on the same database server.

Changing the vCenter database location

If you ever need to locate your vCenter database (this also works for other VMware databases), here are a few ways to get what you need. These methods do not require you to log directly into the SQL database.

This first method will work for the vCenter, View Composer, and the Update Manager database:

1. Log into vCenter Server using an administrator account.

2. Open the `regedit` browser by going to **Start | Run**.

3. Browse through the registry and locate `HKEY_LOCAL_MACHINE\SOFTWARE\ODBC\ODBC.INI`.

4. Choose the database that you are trying to find the location of.

5. Find the string name **Server**. This will contain the name of the server and the location of the database.

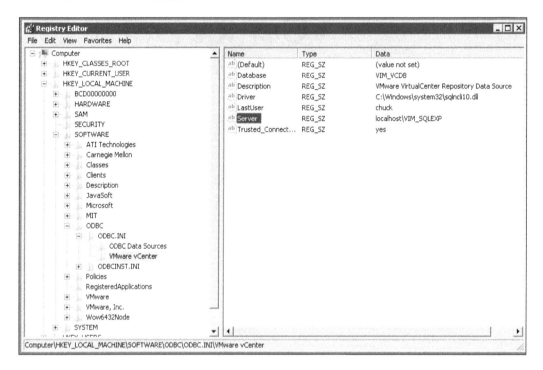

6. Select the entry that has the database you're trying to locate. Now, find the string called **Server**. This will have the server name along with the database, which contains the database name.

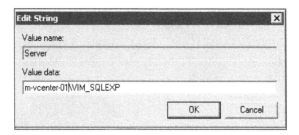

This second method also requires access to vCenter Server. Log in using an administrator account:

1. Use Windows Explorer and go to `c:\ProgramData\VMware\ VmwareVirtualCenter` (this is a hidden folder).

2. Use the notepad or your favorite text editor to open `vcdb.properties`.

3. Locate the line that contains **url=** and you will find the information you are looking for.

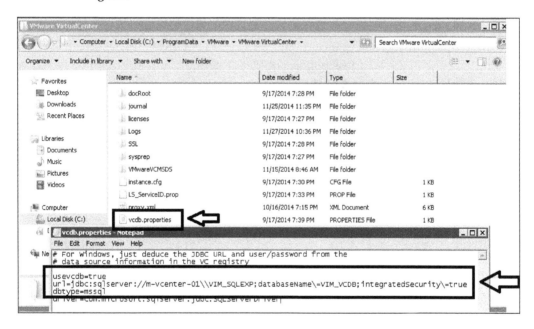

Growing the vCenter Server database

You should always monitor the growth of your vCenter database. The database is collecting and storing information from the vSphere environment. Most of the database's growth is normally due to:

- Logging events
- Logging tasks that were executed
- Collection of performance data
- Wrong recovery settings
- Wrong DB sizing (especially Oracle)

Performance data normally causes the greatest amount of growth but when you are troubleshooting growth problems, make sure that you know the source of the growth. One method to validate the source of database growth is to read the *Determining where growth is occurring in the VMware vCenter Server database* document, found at http://kb.vmware.com/kb/1028356.

There are times when truncating the database information is necessary. This should only be an option if you can determine the source of growth. Make sure you are in compliance with the business policies on data retention, and after you have determined that you are going to truncate the data, review the *Purging Old Data from the database used by VMware vCenter Server* document, found at http://kb.vmware.com/selfservice/microsites/search.do?language=en_US&cmd=displayKC&externalId=1025914.

Reinitializing the vCenter Server database

There might be a time when a reset of the vCenter Server database is the only solution. As bad as that sounds, here are a few reasons to reinitialize the database:

- Corruption of data
- You need to build a new vCenter Server
- VMware Support requires a rebuild

When you reinitialize the vCenter Server database, it will act as a brand new installed instance. It is taken to its default configuration.

You can reset the database with the following steps. All the data (including all custom fields) will be permanently destroyed. A complete backup of your database is highly recommended before executing these reset steps:

1. Stop the vCenter Server service.

2. Open the command prompt.

3. Change to the folder that contains the program file for vCenter Server. If you installed this using the default folder, it will be found at: C:\Program Files\VMware\Infrastructure\VirtualCenter\.

4. At the command prompt, type and execute the following command:

   vpxd.exe -b

   You can see this command executed in the following screenshot:

Fixing the vCenter Server service and database connection issues

If you find that the vCenter service has stopped or does not start, first try starting the service manually to verify the problem.

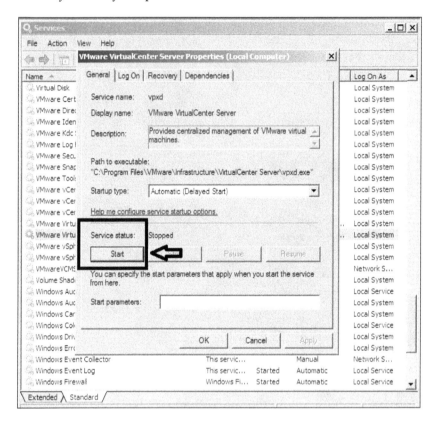

Sometimes, there is a problem with the vCenter Server database that will prevent the service from starting. You can test the ODBC link to verify that a connection can be established. You can also check the Windows log for information on the problem.

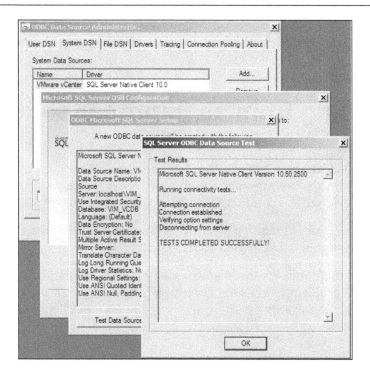

When you need to check vCenter Server's health, use the VMware KB article, *Investigating the Health of a vCenter Server database,* found at `http://kb.vmware.com/selfservice/microsites/search.do?language=en_US&cmd=displayKC&externalId=1003979` to verify the status of the database.

Although this section is about vCenter database troubleshooting, here are a few other items to check after you have verified that your database is fine:

- Review and verify that no changes were made to the OS that vCenter is running on, such as firewalls, virus scanners, and so on.

- Verify whether the vCenter service uses the correct credentials.

- Verify whether the VMware VCMSDS is running (this is the ADAM Writer).

- Make sure ports 902, 443, and 80 (also 1433 for MS SQL and 1521 for Oracle) are not being used by another application. Microsoft IIS could cause conflict with your vCenter on port 80.

- Check the event logs in Windows and search for entries containing the vCenter service.

- Check for `vpxd.log` (vCenter Server log file) found at `C:\ProgramData\VMware\VMware VirtualCenter\Logs` (Windows 2008r2). If you are familiar with Powershell, you can use the **Get-Content vpxd.log –Wait**.

After attempting a manual restart, check the `vpxd.log` file once again. You should find error messages that can help you determine why the vCenter service does not start.

Recovering from an improper shutdown of VCSA

You have installed Virtual Center Server Appliance (VCSA) using the embedded database and there was an improper shutdown of the appliance, so you could experience an error when attempting the startup of your virtual machines.

You could also experience missing information related to the host or virtual machines when you login using the vSphere client.

If you had used the Windows-based vCenter with a local database, you could have solved this problem by connecting to the vCenter Server and resetting (Stop-Start) the vCenter Server service. Then, after logging into the client, the problem is normally resolved.

Remember, the VCSA is an application based on Linux and the methods used to correct these problems are approached differently. You still need to stop and start the vCenter services first. This is accomplished in two ways when using VCSA, by using the Web UI or from the command line of your application.

The Web User Interface (UI) method is completed by opening a complaint browser and entering the address of the vCenter appliance, for example `https://m-vcsa:5480`.

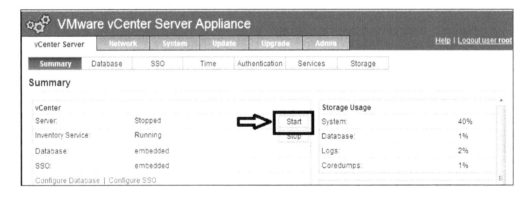

In the vCenter Server screen in the Summary tab, you can **Stop** and **Start** the vCenter Server service from the button.

The second way could be quicker and more comfortable for Linux administrators. Connect to the application and login. The service needs to be `vmware-vpxd` and with a `service vmware-vpxd restart` it is reset.

```
login as: root
VMware vCenter Server Appliance
root@m-vcsa.mills.net's password:
Last login: Fri Nov 28 15:38:49 UTC 2014 from 192.168.2.5 on pts/0
                                          m 192.168.2.5
m-vcsa:~ # service vmware-vpxd restart
Stopping tomcat: success
Stopping vmware-vpxd: success
Shutting down ldap-server..done
Waiting for the embedded database to start up: success
Verifying EULA acceptance: success
Executing pre-startup scripts...
Checking and stopping Inventory Service
Stopping VMware Inventory Service...
Waiting for VMware Inventory Service to exit...
```

Resolving low and no space problems

Running low or actually running completely out of space on the disk in the vCenter environment (Windows-based or appliance) can cause some big problems. Monitoring your system for your disk space amounts, along with many other resource items, will prevent major headaches.

Low space problems

If you find you are low on disk space and are using the embedded database in the VCSA, you can increase your disk space using these steps:

1. Shutting down the VCSA is optional.
2. Add the new hard disk with the size you think you need for the VCSA.
3. Now, power on the VCSA.
4. Log in to the VCSA using the console or SSH.
5. The following command is used to list the disk:

   ```
   fdisk -lu
   ```

You can see this command executed in the following screenshot:

```
m-vcsa:~ # fdisk -lu

Disk /dev/sda: 26.8 GB, 26843545600 bytes
255 heads, 63 sectors/track, 3263 cylinders, total 52428800 sectors
Units = sectors of 1 * 512 = 512 bytes
Sector size (logical/physical): 512 bytes / 512 bytes
I/O size (minimum/optimal): 512 bytes / 512 bytes
Disk identifier: 0x000ade32

   Device Boot      Start         End      Blocks   Id  System
/dev/sda1            2048      272383      135168   83  Linux
/dev/sda2          272384    31743999    15735808   82  Linux swap / Solaris
/dev/sda3   *     31744000    52428799    10342400   83  Linux

Disk /dev/sdb: 107.4 GB, 107374182400 bytes
255 heads, 63 sectors/track, 13054 cylinders, total 209715200 sectors
Units = sectors of 1 * 512 = 512 bytes
Sector size (logical/physical): 512 bytes / 512 bytes
I/O size (minimum/optimal): 512 bytes / 512 bytes
Disk identifier: 0x00000000

   Device Boot      Start         End      Blocks   Id  System
/dev/sdb1            2048    41945087    20971520   83  Linux
/dev/sdb2        41945088    83888127    20971520   83  Linux
/dev/sdb3        83888128   209715199    62913536   83  Linux

Disk /dev/sdc: 5368 MB, 5368709120 bytes
255 heads, 63 sectors/track, 652 cylinders, total 10485760 sectors
Units = sectors of 1 * 512 = 512 bytes
Sector size (logical/physical): 512 bytes / 512 bytes
I/O size (minimum/optimal): 512 bytes / 512 bytes
Disk identifier: 0x00000000

Disk /dev/sdc doesn't contain a valid partition table
m-vcsa:~ #
```

6. Identify the new disk device ID.

7. Access the new disk and the disk utility using the following command:

   `fdisk /dev/sdc`

8. Pressing *N* and *Enter* creates a new partition.

9. Press *P* and *Enter* to create the primary partition.

10. Enter 1, which is the partition number.

11. Choose the default for both the start block and end block.

12. Entering w will write the new partition table to the disk.

13. Now, create the new partition on the newly created disk. You can create an ext3 filesystem by issuing this command:

    `mkfs -t ext3 /dev/sdc1`

14. Under the root, use this command to create a new temporary directory:

    ```
    mkdir /tmp/db
    ```

15. Use this command to mount the newly created disk to /tmp/db, which you created earlier:

    ```
    mount -t ext3 /dev/sdc1 /tmp/db
    ```

16. Stop the services from accessing vPostgres/storage/db with these commands:

    ```
    servicevmware-vpxd stop
    servicevmware-vpostgres stop
    servicevmdird stop
    servicevmware-inventoryservice stop
    ```

17. Copy the files from /storage/db to /tmp/db with the following:

    ```
    cp -a /storage/db/* /tmp/db
    ```

18. Change to the root directory using:

    ```
    cd /
    ```

19. Now un-mount both the original and new disk with the following:

    ```
    umount /dev/sdb3
    umount /dev/sdc1
    ```

20. Mount the newly created disk to /storage/db using:

    ```
    mount -t ext3 /dev/sdc1 /storage/db
    ```

21. When you execute the following, it preserves the new mount to /storage/db:

    ```
    sed -i -e 's#/dev/sdb3#/dev/sdc1#' /etc/fstab
    ```

    At this point, you can reboot the VCSA.

Problems with no space

The **VCSA** summary page gives you an overview of the current status of your environment as it pertains to vCenter. This is a page that you should check on a regular basis.

This **Summary** page will show you what vCenter components are running (or have stopped) and also gives information regarding storage along with other valuable information. Checking this summary can help locate and in some cases, prevent problems.

The **Storage Usage** pane contains important information on the vCenter database. The vCenter section has the information on the type of database you have installed (embedded or external).

Storage Usage	
System:	40%
Database:	100%
Logs:	2%
Coredumps:	1%

One example of this would be when you are unable to connect to the VCSA using your vSphere client. You log in to the application's management console to check things out. You find that your embedded database is 100 percent utilized as we can see in the preceding screenshot. This issue can be caused by exceeding the number of managed hosts and managed virtual machines or the collection of information by vCenter database Retention and Statistics.

The last resort in any situation would be to reinitialize the database—rarely is that an option you want to take. If this is the ONLY solution you have, you need to expand the disk where the database resides. Log in to the VCSA command line.

Run the `mount` command to identify the storage/database.

The following screenshot shows the location of the database on /dev/sdb3. Looking at /dev/sdb3 indicates the second disk (b) and sdb3 shows it to be the third partition.

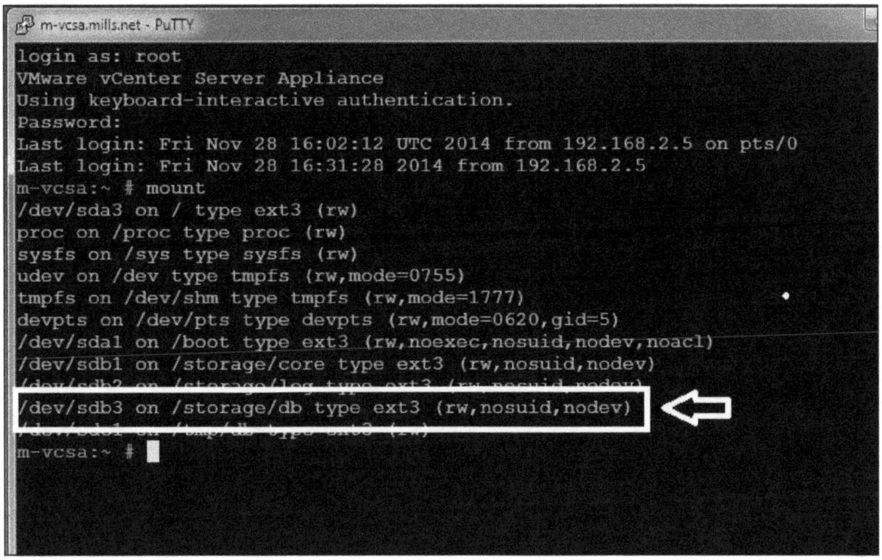

The second hard drive (**VMDK**) needs to have the size increased and reapportioned. Anytime you plan to make a change like this to your virtual machine, you should start with a snapshot. There is an issue with increasing a disk after you snapshot it. The correct way to accomplish this is to increase the disk size and then take the snapshot before you repartition the drive. This gives you a recovery path if something goes wrong. (Thank you Mike Laverick for this useful information).

The following steps will allow you to expand your disk for the vCenter database:

1. Shutdown your VCSA.
2. Use the virtual machine setting to increase disk size.
3. Create a snapshot to allow for a recovery path.
4. At this point, you will need to use your favorite re-partitioning software. You must boot from a DVD or USB device to access the partition and resize it.
5. After the disk has been expanded and re-partitioned, start your VCSA and verify your database has the space it needs to continue to work.

Try this tip when you have low disk space on the Windows version of the vCenter Server disk.

 Sometimes it's not the SQL Database that is using your disk space, but the Windows Update files. Update Manager keeps copies of the updates that are downloaded. Use the `vci-integrity.xml` file located in `C:\Program Files (x86)\VMware\Infrastructure\ Update Manager` for the location of the update files.

Resources for other database issues

There could be a situation where the password on the account used to log in to the database has changed but the registry password has not. This can be corrected by referring to the article, *Changing the vCenter Server database user ID and password*, found at `http://kb.vmware.com/selfservice/microsites/search. do?language=en_US&cmd=displayKC&externalId=1006482`.

Authenticating the database could be a problem if you have imported an instance into the database from another. In this case, the Microsoft article *How to transfer logins and passwords between instances of SQL Server*, will be helpful, which can be found at `http://support.microsoft.com/kb/246133`.

If, for whatever reason, the user was not granted permission to access the vCenter database, the administrative credentials required for Oracle and SQL Server databases when installing or upgrading the vCenter Server article should help. This can be found at `http://kb.vmware.com/selfservice/microsites/search. do?language=en_US&cmd=displayKC&externalId=1003052`.

When using SQL Server, make sure that the transaction logs of the database for vCenter are part of a regular backup plan. This will give you a recovery option if there are severe problems. See the article *Troubleshooting transaction logs on a Microsoft SQL database server*, found at `http://kb.vmware.com/selfservice/microsites/ search.do?language=en_US&cmd=displayKC&externalId=1003980`.

If you are experiencing excessive growth in your transaction logs, review the *Troubleshooting transaction logs on a Microsoft SQL database server* article, found at `http://kb.vmware.com/selfservice/microsites/search.do?language=en_US& cmd=displayKC&externalId=1003980`.

Lastly, if the vCenter server gets disconnected from SQL Server (Oracle also), you might not have a connection to the database repository. This happens because the database retains locks and it will require you to stop and start (or restart) the Database Server Services as shown many times in this chapter.

Summary

In this chapter, we have covered plenty of information regarding the vCenter server database. If anything, you should realize that there are many issues that can cause administrator problems in the vSphere environment in relation to the database. This chapter covered items pertaining to:

- The location of your vCenter database
- How to research and handle the growth of the vCenter server database
- How to resolve vCenter server service and database connection issues
- What to do when the VCSA has an improper shutdown
- How to resolve low and no space problems, along with what to check in order to prevent space problems
- And, if all else fails, how to reinitialize your vCenter server database

We finished this chapter by providing resources for some other database issues you might encounter in your vSphere environment.

One of the most important issues to watch for is having enough disk space for your database. Your database requires adequate disk space to function correctly. If you are reaching limits for this resource, you will need to free up or obtain more disk space.

The next chapter will cover permissions and settings for the vCenter environment. The single sign on password is very important to vCenter. The chapter shows how to reset or unlock that important password. There are permission differences between VCOps and vCenter and they will be covered, along with how to understand the permission differences. The relationship between AD and vCenter and possible connection problems will be covered.

3
Setting Access and Permissions

The **Single Sign On (SSO)** is a feature of vSphere 5.1 that is an authentication broker and a security token exchange that provides a secure way to access your vSphere environment. The SSO password is essential to the vCenter install. This chapter will show you how to reset or unlock that important password. This chapter also shows how to unlock or reset the password for SSO. It will cover the permission difference between vRealize Suite and vCenter, and explains the permissions between vSphere and vCOps. This chapter will cover the relationship between AD and vCenter and the connection between them.

The list of topics that will be covered in this chapter are:

- SSO administrator password unlock or reset
- AD authentication and importing into vCenter SSO 5.5
- Working with permissions for vCenter and VCOps

Introducing vCenter Single Sign-On

Single Sign-On (**SSO**) for vSphere was introduced in version 5.1. SSO acts as the authentication broker, as well as the security token exchange, and provides a better way to securely access the vSphere environment.

This means, before SSO, you would log in to the vCenter Server and your username and password would be authenticated against your Active Directory (AD) that was setup for the vCenter Server.

Now, beginning with vSphere 5.1 along with SSO, you log in to a security domain instead of logging directly into vCenter. The security domain is created when installing the vSphere environment. So, when you log in to vSphere 5.1, you will pass the authentication to the SSO server. Multiple identity sources can be configured with the server, such as AD and/or **Lightweight Directory Access Protocol (LDAP)**. Previously, you could only authenticate with one Active Directory. When you successfully log on, your username and password will be switched for a security token. The token is used to access your vSphere components, such as vCenter Server, Orchestrator, and any others used in your environment.

With SSO being a mandatory component, it must be installed before other vSphere pieces are installed/upgraded. Despite the fact that SSO is new in version 5.1, you can continue to use vSphere as you have done from the pre-5.1 version. Single Sign-On fits right in and is an additional local service separate from your vCenter Server. As mentioned in *Chapter 1, vCenter Upgrades and Migrations*, VMware will introduce a new component in vSphere 6 called the VMware Platform Services Controller (PSC). SSO was the first component to be converted into the PSC. SSO was first found in vSphere 5.1 and, because it contained some major issues, it forced a rebuild to SSO 2.0 for version 5.5. In the new release of vCenter, vRealize, vRealize Automation, and vCloud Director can now use the shared PSC component.

The added benefits of SSO are that it brings administration to many of the vSphere-managed environments. During the installation of the vCenter Server, you can choose to install a vCenter SSO server that provides the ability to administer multiple vCenter Servers. This also includes other components of the centralized vCenter SSO source that authenticate to the SSO. This gives a central look to all your vCenter servers using version 5.0 and newer and allows administration. You also have the option to define queries that search through the multiple vCenter Servers. This was accomplished using Linked Mode in the past.

Unlocking and resetting the SSO administrator password

There may come a time when you are unable to log in to the vSphere Web Client with your administrator credentials to the single SSO server. You can see the error in the following screenshot:

The account for the administrator is automatically locked when there are too many login attempts and they all fail. The default number of attempts is three; after that, the account is locked for a certain period of time. The way to fix this issue is to unlock/reset the account. In order to reset the password for the administrator account, you need to remember the originally installed password. Depending on the version of vSphere you are using, you can do one of the following procedures to reset the account.

vCenter SSO Version 5.1

The policy used to lockout SSO is set to unlock the account after 15 minutes. You need to wait 15 minutes or longer, and then log in using the correct credentials. You can read more information regarding the account lockout policies related to vCenter SSO using *Configuring and troubleshooting vCenter Single Sign On password and lockout policies for accounts* article, found at http://kb.vmware.com/selfservice/ microsites/search.do?language=en_US&cmd=displayKC&externalId=2033823.

You can also unlock the account if a session with SSO administrator privileges is still logged in. Log in to the VCSA using the Web Client and use the following process:

1. Click on **Home**.
2. From the (**Example**) tab, select **Administration**.
3. Select **Users and Groups** found under **Single Sign-On**.

4. Right-click on the problem account and click on **Unlock**.

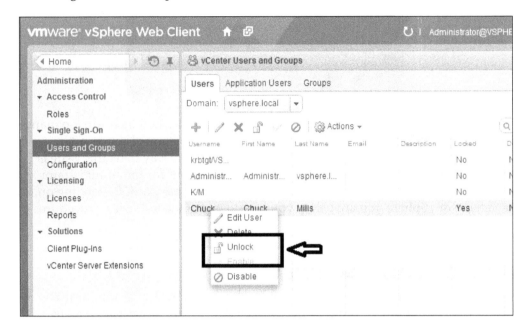

If you find yourself in an emergency situation because the default policies, for some reason, were changed, you have the option to reset the password that unlocks the account. Understand that resetting the password has no effect on the master password that is set up for vCenter SSO 5.1. The master password used by SSO is stored in the database and re-installing from the beginning is the only way to change the SSO master password. The following procedure will generate a secondary password that `administrator@system-domain` will use. Your master password will stay the same as installed.

Log in as the administrator on the SSO server. Open a Command Prompt and go to `SSOInstallDirectory\utils`. The location, if you used the defaults, is `C:\Program Files\VMware\Infrastructure\SSOServer\utils`.

Use the following command:

```
rsautil reset-admin-password
```

Enter the master password at the prompt.

Use the password you chose for the SSO administrator during your installation. If the password has changed, the master password is still the original one you selected. If the command does not prompt you for the master password, you need to use the following command:

```
rsautil reset-admin-password --master-pwd "master_password"
--admin-name admin --admin-pwd new_password
```

Input the SSO administrator name that needs the password reset. Enter your new password for the selected user and confirm for the second time. The new password is checked to make sure it is compliant with the VMware list of supported characters. If everything works, you will see **Password reset successfully**.

Resetting the administrator password with VCSA 5.1

Log in as `root`; from the command line, go to `/usr/lib/vmware-sso/utils` and run this command:

```
./rsautil reset-admin-password
```

Input the master password at the prompt. Input the SSO administrator name that needs the password reset. Type in your new password for the selected user and confirm for the second time. The new password is checked to make sure it is compliant with the VMware list of supported characters. If everything works, you will see **Password reset successfully**.

vCenter Single Sign-On for version 5.5

Version 5.5 lockout policy is the same as in version 5.1: the lockout policy for SSO is set to unlock the account after 15 minutes. You need to wait for that much time or more before logging in using the correct credentials. You can find more information on lockout policies related to vCenter SSO using *Configuring and troubleshooting vCenter Single Sign On password and lockout policies for accounts* article, found at `http://kb.vmware.com/selfservice/microsites/search.do?language=en_US&cmd=displayKC&externalId=2033823`.

You can also unlock the account if a session with SSO administrator privileges is still logged in using the following process:

1. Click on **Home**.
2. From the (**Example**) tab, select Administration.
3. Select **Users and Groups** found under **Single Sign-On**.
4. Right-click on the problem account and click on **Unlock**.

If you find yourself in an emergency situation because the default policies for some reason were changed, you have the option to reset the password and fix the locked account. To reset the `administrator@vsphere.local` password, use a domain administrator account to log in to the vCenter Server. If SSO was installed on a separate server from your vCenter, then log in to the SSO server.

1. Open an admin Command Prompt. Then go to `c:\>cd Program Files\ VMware\Infrastructure\VMware\CIS\vmdird`.

2. Open the service tool `vdcadmintool` using the following command:

   >vdcadmintool.exe

   After the console loads it will look like the following screenshot:

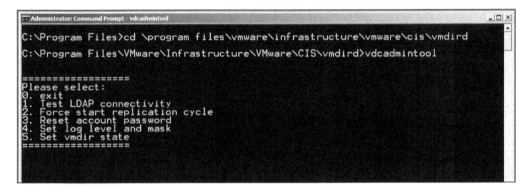

3. Choose option three, that is, `Reset account password`.

4. When you receive the prompt for the Account DN, enter the following command:

   cn=Administrator,cn=users,dc=vSphere,dc=local

   This will generate a new password to be used; log in to the `administrator@ vSphere.local` account. Remember, passwords are case sensitive. The following screenshot shows the new generated password:

```
==================
Please select:
0. exit
1. Test LDAP connectivity
2. Force start replication cycle
3. Reset account password
4. Set log level and mask
5. Set vmdir state
==================

3
   Account DN: cn=Administrator,cn=users,dc=vSphere,dc=local
New password is -
M1Xp<}qBl*<JsI7B3l}1
```

Resetting the administrator password when using VCSA 5.6

Resetting the `administrator@vsphere.local` password on the VCSA 5.6 begins by connecting, either by using SSH or the console.

Open the service tool `vdcadmintool` using the following command:

/usr/lib/vmware-vmdir/bin/vdcadmintool

This console loads as follows:

```
192.168.2.11 - PuTTY
Using keyboard-interactive authentication.
Password:
Last login: Wed Dec 10 08:33:53 UTC 2014 from 192.168.2.5 on pts/0
Last failed login: Wed Dec 10 09:52:45 UTC 2014 from 192.168.2.5 on ssh:notty
There were 2 failed login attempts since the last successful login.
Last login: Wed Dec 10 09:52:48 2014 from 192.168.2.5
m-vcsa:~ # /usr/lib/vmware-vmdir/bin/vdcadmintool


==================
Please select:
0. exit
1. Test LDAP connectivity
2. Force start replication cycle
3. Reset account password
4. Set log level and mask
5. Set vmdir state
==================
```

Follow the process we outlined for vCenter 5.5.

Expired passwords in vSphere 5.1

Your vCenter SSO passwords will expire after 365 days. This includes the `admin@ system-domain` password. When your password for SSO has expired, you will see the following error:

Web Client: provided credentials are not valid

On checking the `vsphere_client_virgo.log`, you will see:

SOAP fault javax.xml.ws.soap.SOAPFaultException: Authentication failed

The administrator for SSO has the ability to change expired passwords for the System-Domain users. Use the SSO administrator account along with the `ssopass` command-line tool, and reset the expired password using the following steps:

1. Select the Windows host where vCenter SSO is installed and open an admin command prompt to run the following:

   ```
   SET JAVA_HOME=C:\Program Files\VMware\Infrastructure\jre
   ```

2. The preceding path is the JRE default path for vCenter Server 5.1. You will then go to the `ssolscli` directory using the following:

   ```
   cd C:\Program Files\VMware\Infrastructure\SSOServer\ssolscli
   ```

3. Once you are in the folder, execute the following command:

   ```
   ssopass -d https://FQDN_of_SSO_server:7444/lookupservice/sdk
   username
   ```

4. Insert your current password, even if it has expired.

5. Insert your password again to confirm it.

If you are using the VCSA, use the following steps to reset the password:

1. Log in to the application as root and go to the following location:

   ```
   /usr/lib/vmware-sso/bin
   ```

2. Execute the following command:

   ```
   ./ssopass -d https://FQDN_of_SSO_server:7444/lookupservice/sdk
   username
   ```

3. Insert the current password, even if it has expired.

4. Insert your new password, and insert it again to confirm.

VMware vCenter server 5.5 U1c release SSO and VCAC

VMware vCenter Server 5.5 U1c has been released and brings interoperability with vRealize Automation along with fixing issues as they relate to SSO. As always, before you upgrade, review the VMware Product Interoperability Matrix (http://partnerweb.vmware.com/comp_guide2/sim/interop_matrix.php) to verify whether the vSphere components you are using are compatible.

To upgrade the VCSA using the management interface (https:// IP Address:5480):

1. Select the **Update** tab.
2. Click on the **Check Updates** button.
3. Click on the **Install Updates** button.

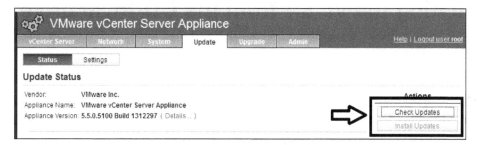

 Take note of your version. vCenter Server 5.5 U1c had an issue with backslashes in the administrator@vSphere.local password. The following information regarding VMware backslashes and SSO is taken from VMware:

> *"To resolve this issue, restart the installer and set a valid password without the backslash (\) character at the end for administrator@vsphere.local."*

This is fixed in the later versions.

Updating the VCSA from a zipped update bundle

When the Internet access is restricted, you can still provide the updates from a zipped update bundle using the following steps:

1. Download the update bundle from the http://www.vmware.com/in website.
2. On an internal web server, create a repository directory.

3. Extract the zipped bundle into the repository directory.

4. Log in to the VCSA management interface using port `5480`.

5. In the **Update** tab, click on **Settings**.

6. Choose the specified repository.

7. Enter the URL of the repository you created.

   For example, if you created the repository directory `vcsa_update`, the URL should be something like `http://your_web_server.company.com/vcsa_update`.

8. Select **Save Settings**.

9. Click on **Status**.

10. Under **Actions** tab, click on **Install Updates**.

Updating the VCSA from the CD-ROM drive

You can update the VCSA from an ISO using a virtual CD-ROM drive with the help of the following steps:

1. Download the VCSA update ISO file from `http://www.vmware.com/in`.

2. Edit the VM setting to connect the VCSA CD-ROM to the ISO file you downloaded.

3. Log in to VCSA management interface using port `5480`.

4. In the **Update** tab, click on **Settings**.

5. Under **Update Repository**, select **Use CD-ROM Updates**.

6. Click on **Save Settings.**

7. Then, click on **Status**.

8. Under **Actions** tab, click on **Install Updates**.

Adding additional Active Directory authentication in vCenter SSO 5.5

As noted a few times in the previous chapter, SSO was rewritten in the release of vSphere 5.5. With that rewrite there is a new identity type referred to as AD/**Integrated Windows Authentication**. This new feature, unlike the old vSphere 4.x / 5.0 authentications, will work without the need to choose the AD controllers directly. This makes the entire process much easier to use. This section will show you how to enable the AD authentication with vSphere 5.5 SSO. This method allows the management of AD users and groups. The solution works for both the vCenter Server 5.5 (Windows based), along with the VCSA.

To enable AD, use the following process:

1. Open the web client (`https:// address of your vCenter Server:9443/vsphere-client`).

2. Log in as `administrator@vsphere.local`.

> If using Windows, the password is input during installation. If using the VCSA, the password is `vmware`.

3. Select **Home** tab.

4. Then, select **Administration**.

5. Select SSO **User and Groups**

6. Select **Configuration** and then select the **Identity Sources** tab.

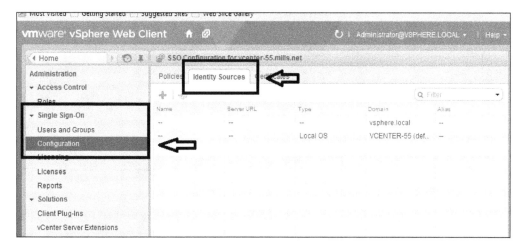

If you do not see the SSO configuration, there is a good chance you did not use the `administrator@vsphere.local` account or SSO administrator account.

7. Click on the plus sign (**+**) to add the new identity.

8. Select the identity source type by going to **Identity Sources** tab.

9. Then, select the **Active Directory (Integrated Windows Authentication)** option.

10. Then click on **OK**.

Your AD should appear in **Identity source type:**. From this point on, the assignment of vCenter permissions (**Groups and Users**) are used through Active Directory. When you use Integrated Windows Authentication, any of your trusted domains will also be available. This should be similar to the methods used in version 4.x and 5.0.

Choose the AD and click on the arrow in the globe button to select your default domain.

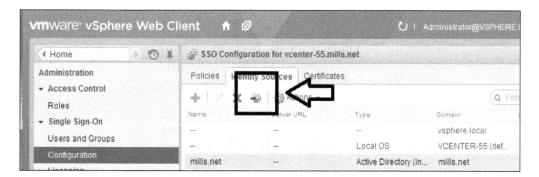

You will get a warning stating, **This will alter your current default domain. Do you want to proceed?**, which is normal due to the fact that you can only select one default domain.

Now you are going to set permissions and authentication used against AD, and vCenter Server 5.5 will go through SSO. If you want other users to make changes to the SSO configuration (other than administrator@vsphere.local), you need to include the users in your SSO Administrator Group.

Permissions for vCenter and vCenter Operations Manager

One of the difficulties for a new administrator is exactly how to control access to the objects that any particular user can see within the vCenter Operations Manager (now vRealize). This starts with the misconception that a user must be a full vSphere Administrator to use vRealize. This thought is incorrect and by the end of this section, things will be clear.

Let's start by setting up the vRealize access. Begin by creating a clone of the existing read-only role to a new role, for example, **vCOps Read-only**.

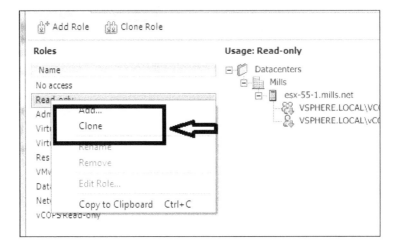

Then, edit the newly created role (**vCOPS Read-only**), and add-in global permissions to vCOps Manager User, as shown in the following screenshot:

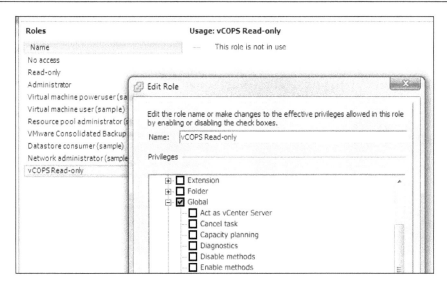

If you fail to assign the vCOPS User global permission for the vCenter object, it causes the **User not authorized** error when logging in.

Now, we need to set the permission (vCOPS User) for the vCenter object by assigning a user to the new **vCOPS Read-only** role we just created. Use the hierarchy of the vCenter object and turn off propagation. This can be changed if the user requires visibility to the entire infrastructure. Refer to the following screenshot:

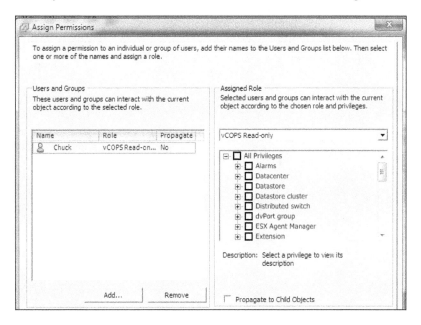

Apply any other permission needed by the user for any other selected locations.

The following screenshot shows an example of the permissions applied for the user with **VCOps Read-only** at the root object with propagation disabled. A second cluster (**Linthicum**) with propagation is also enabled.

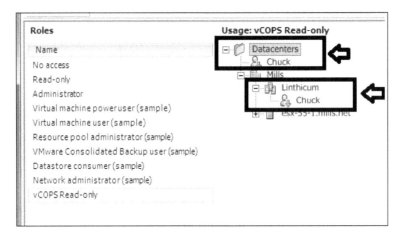

The user can see only the **Linthicum** cluster as shown in the preceding screenshot, and cannot see **Kingbrook**, for instance. The following screenshot shows that there is a second cluster in the environment:

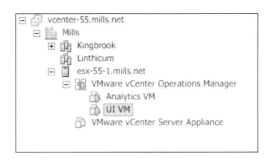

Tips for troubleshooting vCenter permissions

Here are a few items to consider when troubleshooting vCenter permissions. There are times when you will experience strange errors when permissions are not applied correctly, for example, *user not authorized* or *incorrect username/password* when the user tries to login. This can happen when the user has permissions assigned in a variety of levels. Check all levels (vCenter object, Cluster, and the Data Center), then make sure read-only role is set up correctly at the cluster level. To avoid issues like these, be sure that the level of permissions across your users is consistent. Pay close attention to the top layers of permissions. When giving account rights to the vCenter object, make sure it has vCOps User access.

Summary

This chapter reviewed the importance of the SSO, and how to reset or unlock the password, along with some of the issues that you might face. This chapter also covered the relationship between AD and vCenter, and how to setup AD with vCenter for both the Windows based and virtual appliance. Finally, we covered the permission differences between vCOps and vCenter, and how to set up the permissions for users.

The next chapter will cover Operations Manager and how you can use it to monitor parts of the vSphere environments. We will cover how Operations Manager can identify the I/O intensive virtual machines. The chapter explores how vCenter uses Java and the configurations that provide the best performance. The chapter helps the administrator recover from issues that occur when a change is made to vCenter and when the performance information is not being displayed.

4
Monitoring and Performance Considerations

The topics covered will show you how to monitor some of the performance areas of the vSphere environments. There will be an overview of disk I/O performance, and how to use vSphere to identify the I/O intensive virtual machines. This chapter will also explore how vCenter uses Java, and how it should be configured to obtain the best performance. This chapter will help the administrator recover from the issues that occur when a change is made to vCenter and when the performance information does not get displayed.

Here is a list of the topics that will be covered in the chapter:

* Overview of disk I/O performance
* Pinpointing the most I/O intensive virtual machines
* Changing Java memory usage for performance
* Fixing the issue with performance data not appearing on vCenter

Overview of disk I/O performance

With the ever-increasing density of physical ESXi hosts hosting virtual machines, it is easy to understand the increase in disk I/O activity across the server's disk subsystem. This, coupled with certain application workloads that are sensitive to I/O latency, makes this a resource to watch.

When you consider all the resources (computer, memory, storage, and networking) that are needed to create the vSphere environment, storage is normally the slowest resource and in some cases, it is a complex resource to understand. When storage problems, such as bottlenecks occur, they are most likely to have a negative impact on virtual machines.

Most storage performance issues can be the result of a configuration problem (or the result of investing in the wrong HW), and care should be taken during the installation or updating of the storage environment. Using the highest performing disks and controllers with top speed connections will improve the storage performance of your virtual environment. Along with the speed of the disk, consider the type of disk drive, and other settings, such as the RAID type. Pairing the local SATA drives with ESXi is possible and it is cheaper, but if you have applications with high performing requirements, then you would be better off selecting either Ultra320 SCSI drives or SAS disks. Also, there are current solutions such as, VMware VSAN (Virtual Storage Area Network), all SSD storages and the vFlash options to help you in this area.

If you are using local storage, to ascertain the possibility of a test and development environment, you can check if your disk controllers support multiple channels on the card. This way, you can split your disks across multiple channels to achieve a performance improvement. You might also have the option of installing multiple disk controllers, and therefore, you may install additional disks on your host server. This gives you the ability to split your file system, and it also allows you to strategically place the VMs based on the needs of I/O resources.

Getting ESXi host and VM disk I/O information

Prior to virtualization, you could measure the storage performance capability of a single computer with the help of throughput. Throughput is the average number of megabytes transferred within a measured period of a specific file size. Now, with virtualization and with several VMs on a physical host, using throughput for this purpose might not be accurate enough. Measuring the storage solution's ability of handling all those packets of data requests from the many VMs requires another method of measurement, which is IOPS (Input/Output Operations per Second). IOPS measures the storage system's performance based on the number of operations per second with a different (better) way of measuring the consumption of the guest VMs within a VMware environment.

The following section will show you how to get the disk usage and performance information from the vSphere environment. This information is valuable either for troubleshooting the VM issue or for the sizing and planning of a new storage system. The information could be used to determine whether a solution, such as adding more drives could help in solving the problem and one could avoid buying a new system.

Getting information using the vSphere client

Use the vSphere client and follow this procedure for collecting the information:

1. Connect to vCenter by using a Windows based Client.

2. Select the ESXi host.

3. Click on the **Performance** tab.

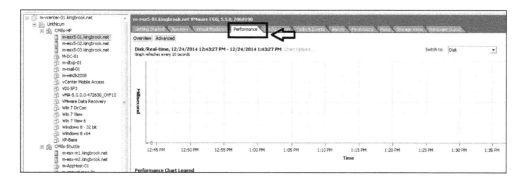

4. Click on the **Advanced** button at the top.

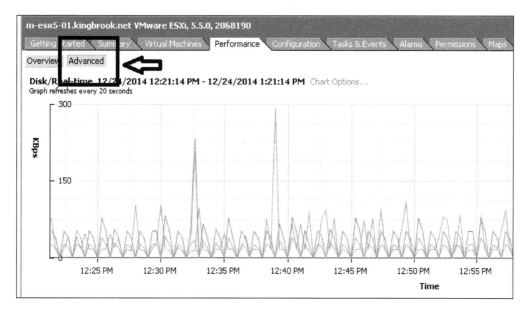

5.   Using the drop down box, select **Disk**.

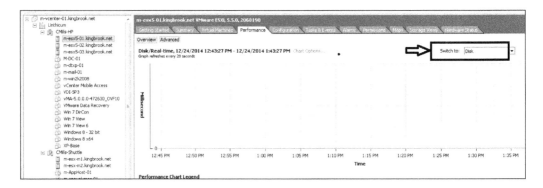

 You can see the real-time read and write stats in Kbps, and you can also see the **Latest**, **Maximum**, **Minimum**, and **Average** values in the default view.

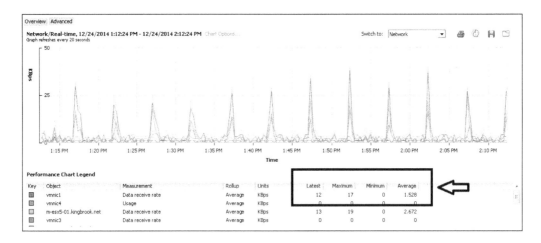

6.   Use the **Chart Options...** for changing the historical data.

7.   Use the **Chart options...** to provide the following order of selections for historical data:

  ○   **Real-time**

  ○   **Past day**

  ○   **Past week**

  ○   **Past month**

- ° **Past year**
- ° **Custom**

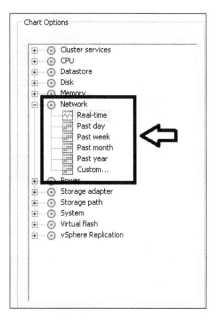

8. Use the **Chart Type** option to select the **Stacked graph** option or the **Stacked Graph (Per VM)** option.

9. Click on **Apply**, and then click on **OK** to implement the changes made to collect the requested information.

Getting information using the service console ESXi Shell

You can also collect the information regarding the I/O performance by using the `esxtop` command line. In this, you would connect to your host by using an SSH client, such as PuTTY or mRemote. Once you connect successfully to your client, start `esxtop` to watch the disk usage from service console ESXi Shell.

After you log in to the service console ESXi Shell, execute the following steps:

1. After you log in to the service console ESXi Shell, type `esxtop`.

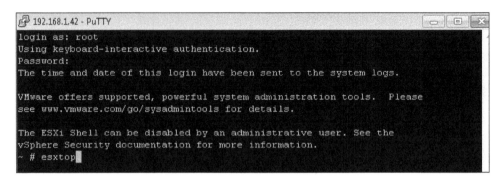

2. To change from default CPU stats to ESX disk adapter stats, press the *D* key.

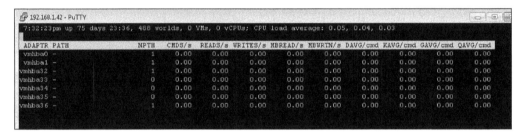

3. To change the view to see ESX disk device stats, press the *U* key.

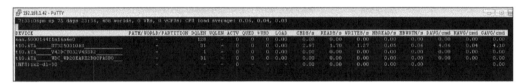

4. To change the view to see ESX disk VM stats, press the *V* key.

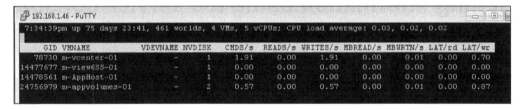

5. To see help at any time while using `esxtop`, press the *H* key.

```
192.168.1.46 - PuTTY
Esxtop version 5.5
Secure mode Off

Esxtop: top for ESX

These single-character commands are available:

^L       - redraw screen
space    - update display
h or ?   - help; show this text
q        - quit

Interactive commands are:

fF       Add or remove fields
oO       Change the order of displayed fields
s        Set the delay in seconds between updates
#        Set the number of instances to display
W        Write configuration file ~/.esxtop50rc
k        Kill a world
e        Expand/Rollup VM vscsi Statistics
L        Change the length of the NAME field
l        Limit display to a single group

Sort by:
         r:READS/s       w:WRITES/s
         R:MBREAD/s      T:MBWRTN/s
         N:Default
Switch display:
         c:cpu           i:interrupt      m:memory       n:network
         d:disk adapter  u:disk device    v:disk VM      p:power mgmt

Hit any key to continue:
```

6. To exit `esxtop`, press the *Q* key.

Pinpointing the most I/O-intensive virtual machines

You can use the vSphere disk performance charts to monitor the disk I/O usage for your hosts, clusters, and virtual machines. Review the information given here to help you in troubleshooting and correcting some of the disk I/O problems.

The virtual machine (VM) disk usage percentage (%) and the I/O data counters give you information on the average disk usage of a VM. You can use the counters to monitor the disk usage trends. One of the best ways to find out if your environment has any disk performance problems is by monitoring the disk latency data counters, using the advanced performance charts and reviewing the statistics, as explained in the following section.

After you choose the **Advanced** tab in **Customize Performance Charts**, choose the chart option. To determine the average amount of time that VMkernel spends on processing every SCSI command (in milliseconds), you will use the **kernelLatency** data counter.

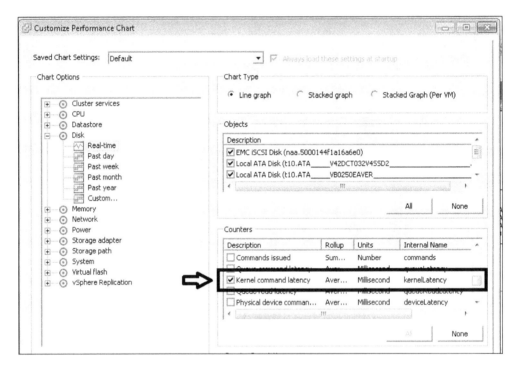

To get the best performance, this value should be between zero and one millisecond. If you find the value to be more than four milliseconds, it would mean that the VMs on your ESXi host are sending more storage throughput than your configuration can support. In this case, you would check the CPU usage, and then increase the queue depth.

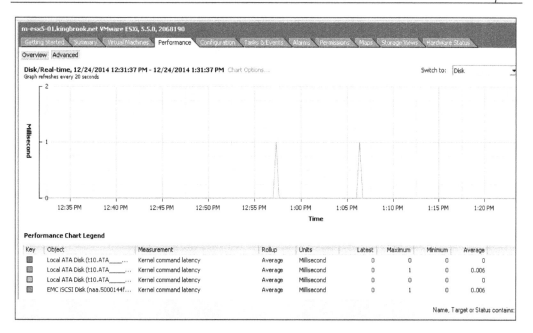

The **deviceLatency** data counter measures the average amount of time it takes to complete an SCSI command received from a physical device (in milliseconds).

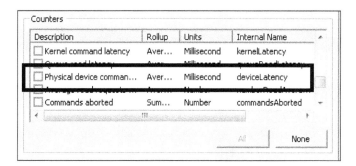

This is a little more hardware dependent, but the values that are greater than 15 milliseconds could indicate problems with the storage array (outside the ESXi host). You could either add more diskspace to the **logical unit number** (**LUN**), or try to move (by using Storage vMotion) the VMDK to another volume that has more spindles. Check your values after completing the action to verify that you have reduced the number. You can find additional information at http://kb.vmware. com/selfservice/microsites/search.do?language=en_US&cmd=displayKC&ext ernalId=1008205.

Note that, using SVMotion is more intrusive to the vSphere environment than using VMotion, because SVMotion copies significant amounts of data. When using VMotion, the files of the virtual machine do not get copied and VM moves from host to host. whereas SVMotion moves the VM from host to host, so it could degrade the performance of VM.

To find the average time taken per SCSI command in the VMkernel queue, you should use the **queueLatency** data counter measures.

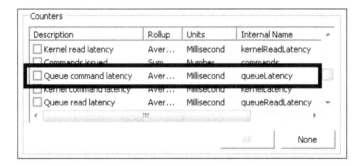

This value should always be zero. Anything but zero for this value would indicate that the workload is too high for the array and that it cannot process data fast enough.

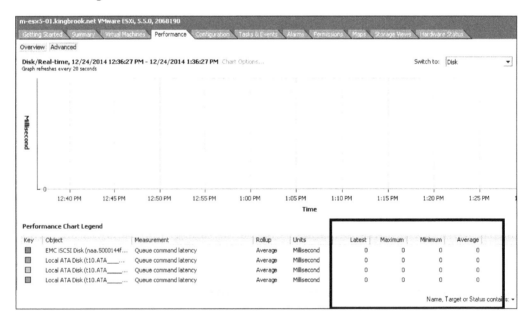

Other items to increase disk I/O performance

The previous section showed you how to use vCenter to pinpoint some of the more I/O intensive virtual machines in order to make the necessary adjustments to those VMs. Here are a few general practices which you can put to use for the overall configuration of the vSphere environment to either avoid or resolve the I/O problems:

- Increase the virtual machine memory. This allows the operating system (OS) to have more caching, which reduces the I/O activity. If you do not have the additional host resources to accomplish this, then you should increase the physical memory of your host. For example, by increasing the memory, the databases could utilize the system memory to cache the data and reduce disk access. You can check the swapping stats in the OS to verify that the virtual machines have adequate memory and, if needed, increase the guest memory. Make sure not to increase the memory to the point that it leads to excessive host memory swapping.

- Antivirus scans (most of the time), by default, scan all the files on the system. You could see performance improvements by disabling the scanning of the VMDK and VMEM files when performing a scheduled scan. You could also consider VMware vShield Endpoint, which provides virtualization and security protection of the endpoint VMs by using a secure virtual appliance to offload the antivirus processing.

- Most of the storage array vendors have their own set of tools to help determine the health of their arrays. You could use the information provided by the vendor tools to help troubleshoot and resolve some of the common issues with storage.

- VMware provides features, such as Storage vMotion (SVMotion) to help balance the I/O-intensive VM across your storage environment. Make sure that you are using this and that you have configured it correctly. Spread the heavily used storage across the different LUNs accessed by the different adapters and use separate queues for each adapter to improve your disk efficiency.

- Use the vendor tools or any other vendor resources to make sure that the HBAs, NFS mount options, and RAID controllers are configured for optimal use. Use reports and verify that items, such as queue depths and cache settings on the RAID controllers are configured as per your need.

- When you have I/O intensive virtual machines, you could separate the VM's OS disk drive from its system page file and place it back when you eliminate the spindle contention. This will help during the high-usage period of the VM.

- If you find that the combined disk I/O is higher than the capacity of a single **hot bus adapter** (**HBA**), then look at the use of multipathing or multiple links.

- If you know that the VM is going to be I/O intensive, if you create virtual disks, choose the pre-allocated (thick disk) option. Allocating all the disk space up front circumvents the problem of performance degradation, which is associated with reassigning additional disk space. This also dodges the problems associated with disk fragmentation.

- Consider third-party SSD Caching products that "hold" the most frequently accessed data on the low latency storage.

- Store the API integration in the ESXi server.

- Store the vSWAP redirection on tier one storage.

- Balance the VMs per LUN, the ESXi per cluster, and the LUNS per ESXi host.

Changing Java memory usage for performance

According to the *vSphere Installation and Setup Guide*, the vCenter Server includes several Java services in the installation of components, such as vCenter Management Web services, Inventory Services, and Profile-Driven Storage Services. When you install the vCenter Server, you get the option to select the size of the vCenter Server inventory for allocating memory for these services. The inventory size determines the maximum **Java Virtual Machine** (**JVM**) heap settings for these services. If, for some reason, this is not set correctly, then it could affect the vCenter performance.

The following image shows the default values for the JVM heap settings in vSphere. For version 5.5, table 2.5 of the *vSphere Installation and Setup Guide* can be found on page 20 at http://pubs.vmware.com/vsphere-55/topic/com.vmware.ICbase/PDF/vsphere-esxi-vcenter-server-552-installation-setup-guide.pdf.

JVM Heap Settings for vCenter Server

vCenter Server Inventory	VMware VirtualCenter Management Webservices (tc Server)	Inventory Service	Profile-Driven Storage Service	Overall minimum memory recommendation
Small inventory (1-100 hosts or 1-1000 virtual machines) 51	512MB	3GB	12GB	16GB
Medium inventory (100-400 hosts or 1000-4000 virtual machines)	512MB	6GB	2GB	24GB
Large inventory (More than 400 hosts or 4000 virtual machines)	1024MB	12GB	4GB	32GB

Use the following procedure if you find that there is a need to change the settings of the services after installation.

Changing the Java heap setting for vCenter

Here are the changes that need to be made in vCenter for adjusting the Java settings (case sensitive):

1. Open Windows Explorer and navigate to `C:\Program Files\VMware\Infrastructure\tomcat\conf`.

2. Use the Notepad to open `wrapper.conf` file.

3. Move to the line `wrapper.java.additional.9=`.

4. Change the setting to the value that you need according to the JVM heap setting mentioned earlier.

5. Save and close the file.

```
wrapper.conf - Notepad
File  Edit  Format  View  Help
#****************************************************************
# wrapper Properties
#****************************************************************
set.CATALINA_HOME=C:\Program Files\Common Files\VMware\VMware vCenter Server - tc Server
set.CATALINA_BASE=C:\Program Files\VMware\Infrastructure\tomcat
set.VIM_LOGDIR=C:\ProgramData\VMware\VMware VirtualCenter\Logs

# Java Main class.  This class must implement the wrapperListener interface
#  or guarantee that the WrapperManager class is initialized.  Helper
#  classes are provided to do this for you.  See the Integration section
#  of the documentation for details.
wrapper.java.mainclass=org.tanukisoftware.wrapper.WrapperSimpleApp

# Java Home
set.JAVA_HOME=C:\Program Files\Common Files\VMware\VMware vCenter Server - Java Components\

# Java Additional Parameters
wrapper.java.additional.1="-Dvim.logdir=%VIM_LOGDIR%"
wrapper.java.additional.2="-Djava.endorsed.dirs=%CATALINA_BASE%\endorsed"
wrapper.java.additional.3="-Dcatalina.base=%CATALINA_BASE%"
wrapper.java.additional.4="-Dcatalina.home=%CATALINA_HOME%"
wrapper.java.additional.5="-Djava.io.tmpdir=%CATALINA_BASE%\temp"
wrapper.java.additional.6="-Djava.util.logging.manager=com.springsource.tcserver.serviceability
wrapper.java.additional.7="-Djava.util.logging.config.file=%CATALINA_BASE%\conf\logging.propert
wrapper.java.additional.9="-Xmx512M"          <===
wrapper.java.additional.11="-Xincgc"
wrapper.java.additional.12="-XX:+ForceTimeHighResolution"
wrapper.java.additional.13="-XX:PermSize=64M"
wrapper.java.additional.14="-XX:MaxPermSize=256M"

# Java Library Path
wrapper.java.library.path.1=%CATALINA_HOME%\bin\winx86_64
wrapper.java.library.path.2=%CATALINA_BASE%\bin\winx86_64
```

Making changes to the vCenter inventory services

Here are the changes that are needed in the vCenter inventory services for adjusting the Java settings:

1. Open Windows Explorer and navigate to C:\Program Files\VMware\ Infrastructure\Inventory Service\conf.

2. Use the Notepad to open wrapper.conf file.

3. Move to the line # Maximum Java Heap Size (in MB).

4. Change the setting to the value that you need according to the JVM heap setting mentioned earlier.

5. Save and close the file.

Making changes to the profile-driven storage services

Here are the changes that need to be made to the profile-driven storage services when adjusting the Java settings:

1. Open Windows Explorer and navigate to `C:\Program Files\VMware\Infrastructure\Profile-Driven Storage\conf`.

2. Use the Notepad to open `wrapper.conf` file.

3. Move to the line `# Maximum Java Heap Size (in MB)`.

4. Change the setting to the value that is needed according to the JVM heap setting mentioned earlier.

5. Save and close the file.

After completing the changes, restart the vCenter services or reboot vCenter to make sure that the changes take effect.

Fixing issues with performance data that do not appear in vCenter

There are some known issues with performance data that do not show for the hosts in vCenter, yet if you directly log in to the host itself, the data will be displayed. This can happen after vCenter is upgraded and, as a result, you may see data on some hosts, while it won't show on others.

There are two methods to resolve this issue.

Method 1 – Log in to the ESXi host directly using the vSphere Client

You need to directly log in to the ESXi host by using the vSphere Client. Do not log in to to vCenter; use the following directions:

1. Click on the **Configuration** tab, along the top window.

2. Then, choose the **Security Profile** option. You will find this under the **Software** section.

3. Click on **Properties...**, which is at the top right section of the **Security Profile** section.

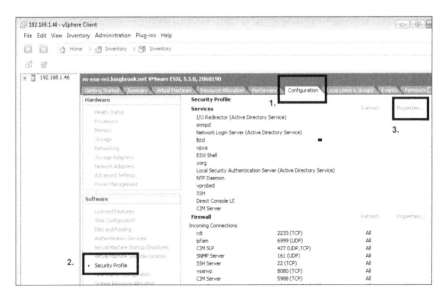

4. Once you open **Service Properties**, select the following options:

    ◦ **vpxa**
    ◦ **Options**
    ◦ **Restart**

This will restart the **vpxa** service.

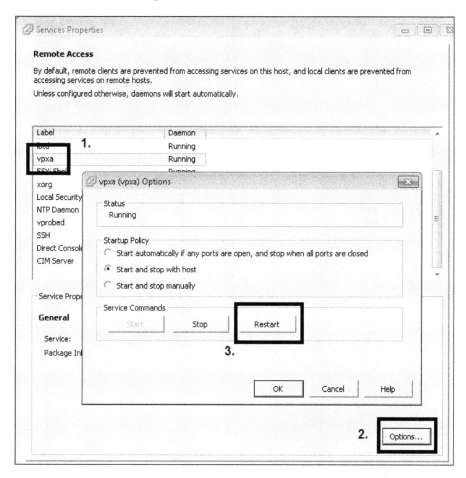

You should wait 15 or 20 minutes before checking the **Performance** tab of the ESXi hosts from vCenter.

Method 2 – Restart the management agent using the Direct Console User Interface

Use PuTTY (a SSH and telnet client) to connect to the ESXi host and login using the root account. Then you can display the Direct Console User Interface by typing dcui at the ESXi shell prompt.

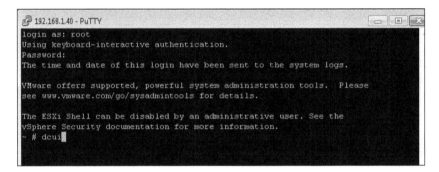

 The DCUI is the screen that you see when you use the ESXi console directly, and the commands outlined here can be used for the same.

After the DCUI screen appears, do the following:

1. Press the *F2* key.

2. You will need to enter the root password again.

3. Use the arrow keys to select **Troubleshooting Mode Options** and press *Enter*.

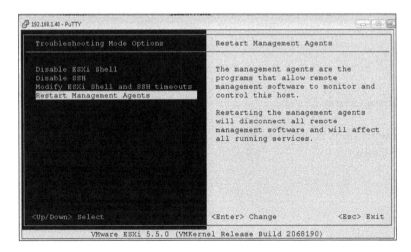

4. Use the arrow keys to select **Restart Management Agents** and press *Enter*.

5. You need to press the *F11* key to confirm that the Management Agent restarts.

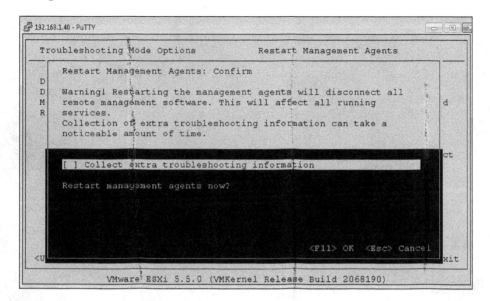

 Note that, restarting the management agent will cause the disconnection of all sessions, and it will temporarily halt all activities of the host. So, restart the agent at an appropriate time.

6. Press *Ctrl* + *C* to quit from DCUI screen.

You can also restart management agent service without using DCUI by using just a shell command. You can use PuTTY to log in to the ESXi host (SSH), and at the shell prompt, type the `/etc/init.d/hostd restart` command.

```
192.168.1.40 - PuTTY
login as: root
Using keyboard-interactive authentication.
Password:
The time and date of this login have been sent to the system logs.

VMware offers supported, powerful system administration tools.  Please
see www.vmware.com/go/sysadmintools for details.

The ESXi Shell can be disabled by an administrative user. See the
vSphere Security documentation for more information.
~ # /etc/init.d/hostd restart
watchdog-hostd: Terminating watchdog process with PID 34199
hostd stopped.
Ramdisk 'hostd' with estimated size of 178MB already exists
hostd started.
~ #
```

You should wait 15 or 20 minutes before checking the **Performance** tab of the ESXi hosts from vCenter, when using the DCUI or the command line option for restarting the agents.

You can find more information regarding the performance data vCenter rollup jobs at http://kb.vmware.com/selfservice/microsites/search.do?language=en_US&cmd=displayKC&externalId=2007388.

Summary

This chapter covered the topics around monitoring the performance considerations for the vSphere environment. There was an overview of the disk I/O, which can have a negative impact on the virtual machines. We discussed what type of reports from vCenter can be used for pinpointing problems. There was a review of how vCenter uses Java, and how to change the configuration to obtain the best performance. The chapter covered the issue of performance data missing from vCenter on the host and how to resolve this problem by using different methods.

The next chapter will cover the troubleshooting of storage devices. Issues, such as deleting the virtual machine snapshot that has locked the files and is preventing the administrator from performing the cleanup, shall be discussed. It will also show how to un-mount an LUN from multiple the ESXi hosts. Using the vCenter Operations for troubleshooting other issues with the storage devices will be discussed.

5
Working with Storage

Many vSphere administrators are thrown into maintaining virtualization storage and are normally not given the time to develop the proper level of knowledge in this area. VM storage is virtualized into **VM disk files** (**VMDKs**), which abstracts storage from the physical storage hardware. **Raw Device Mapping** (**RDM**) provides a mapping file to VMFS volume, which works as a proxy for a physical storage device. Using RDM provides virtual machines a way to access and use a storage device directly. Troubleshooting storage is another important skill needed by the administrator, and this chapter will help with a few storage issues.

The list of topics that will be covered in this chapter are:

- Deleting a virtual machine snapshot that has locked files
- Unmounting a LUN from multiple ESXi hosts
- Using vCenter operations to troubleshoot storage devices

Deleting virtual machine snapshots that have locked files

Here are a few issues you might experience while working with the vSphere environment with regards to snapshots of your virtual machines.

There might be times when you have snapshots created but have the following issues:

- You are unable to have the snapshot committed
- The snapshot commits with no errors and everything looks fine in the snapshot manager, but there are still snapshot disks in the virtual machine's directory that can't be removed

- You experience errors/failures from your backup solution because of the snapshot file that was not deleted during the snapshot commit

If you check the `/var/log/hostd.log` file on the ESXi host, you will find a message similar to the following:

```
If you attempt to remove the datastore, not knowing of the previous
problem you will receive an error similar to this:
The resource '<VMFS-UUID>' is in use.
```

Another snapshot issue you might have running on vSphere 5.0 or above is when you click on the virtual machine's vCenter **Summary** tab:

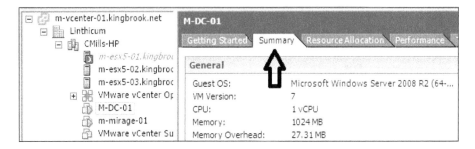

At this point, you are presented with the message **snapshot consolidation required**, but when you try to consolidate, you receive an error message:

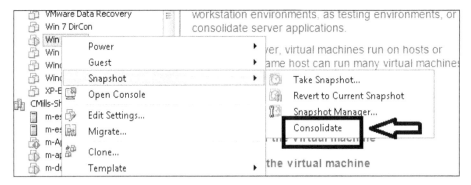

The error you see is similar to the following:

```
Consolidate virtual machine disk files <hostname> Unable to access
file <unspecified filename> since it is locked
```

All of the issues described earlier can happen when backing up a server. A virtual appliance or virtual machine establishes a lock on the underlying virtual machine's base disk (.vmdk) or one of the snapshot files (for example, a .vmsn file). This prevents the snapshot file from being consolidated.

Backup servers and backup appliances (these are components with a virtual environment dedicated to making backups) can create snapshots through the use of vStorage APIs. After the backup is complete, the backup server/appliance makes a request for the snapshot taken for the backup to be deleted and for the data to be merged into the previous disk. If the delete request for the snapshot is issued too soon, then the base disk is locked by the server or appliance performing the backup and therefore, it cannot be deleted. The result of this condition will produce messages similar to these:

- The snapshot deletion process will be terminated
- Snapshot manager has inaccurate or does not have enough information
- The VM will continue to run on the VM's snapshots

Go to `http://kb.vmware.com/selfservice/microsites/search.do?language=en_US&cmd=displayKC&externalId=2007245` to find out more about the issue with snapshot consolidation after backing up a virtual machine fails with the error: **Failed to consolidate disks found here**.

Go to `http://kb.vmware.com/selfservice/microsites/search.do?language=en_US&cmd=displayKC&externalId=2040846` to find out more about the issue with consolidating disks associated with a backup snapshot fails with the error: **The file is already in use found here**.

Troubleshooting the locked files

Now that you understand the possible cause of the locked snapshot files, here are a few resolutions to try and resolve your problem.

Removing the file from a backup virtual appliance

Here's how we remove the file from a backup virtual appliance:

1. Power down the backup server/appliance and prepare to remove the .vmdk file from it.
2. Check the backup server/appliance to make sure it is safe to remove the disk from it.

3. Right-click on the **Backup Appliance Virtual Machine** and click on **Edit Settings**.

4. Check if the affected virtual machine's hard disk is mounted on the backup appliance virtual machine.

5. If the hard disk is mounted, select **Hard disk 1** and select **Remove** from the virtual machine options:

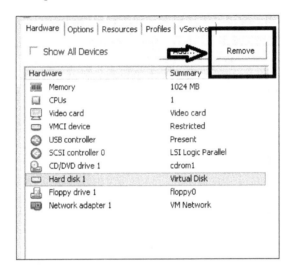

 Do not select the **Delete** option as this will result in data loss.

6. Click on **OK** to exit.

Performing the Delete All action from the Snapshot Manager

Create a new snapshot of the affected virtual machine by right-clicking on the VM and choosing **Clone...**:

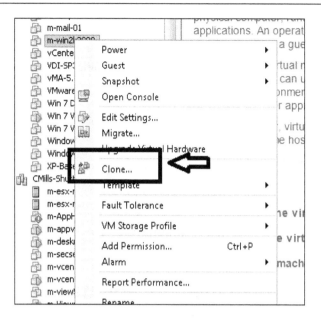

Then, perform the **Delete All** action from the snapshot manager to consolidate all the snapshots:

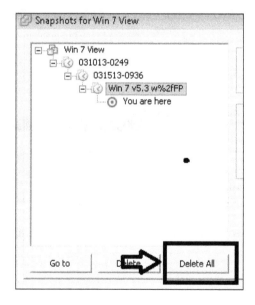

If you are using vSphere 5.0 or above, you can attempt to consolidate without creating a new snapshot first. Right-click on **Virtual machine** and navigate to **Snapshot | Consolidate**. If this fails, try again by creating a new snapshot, as mentioned earlier.

If the delete process is successful, check the VM's folder to make sure all the snapshots are consolidated. If the delete process fails, check the lock messages again to determine which host has a lock on the `name-flat.vmdk` file or the `name-delta.vmdk` file. For more information, see the *Determining if a virtual disk is attached to another virtual machine (1003656)* page at `http://kb.vmware.com/selfservice/microsites/search.do?language=en_US&cmd=displayKC&externalId=1003656`.

If you find that the disk is attached to another VM, use the method described earlier to remove it.

Restarting the management agents

If you continue to receive lock messages, perform a restart of the management agents on the ESXi host where the VM is running by using the management console, as shown in the following screenshot:

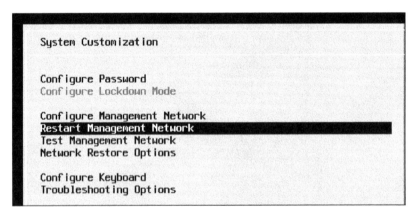

You can accomplish the same task using the command line, as shown in the following image:

```
~ #
~ # etc/init.d/hostd restart
watchdog-hostd: Terminating watchdog process with PID 33776
hostd stopped.
Ramdisk 'hostd' with estimated size of 176MB already exists
hostd started.
~ # etc/init.d/vpxa restart
watchdog-vpxa: Terminating watchdog process with PID 34476
vpxa stopped.
~ #
```

Moving the Virtual Machine and rebooting the host

If you cannot determine which process or VM is holding the lock on the file, you can try migrating the running VM off the ESXi host that is holding the lock and rebooting the host. If you cannot reboot the host, then try cloning the disk with the problem to create a new disk. Use the following procedure:

1. Power off the virtual machine with the locked disk.

2. Clone the latest snapshot disk (that is, `name-000003.vmdk`) from the command line. Connect to your host using an SSH client, such as Putty or mRemote, and navigate to the folder that contains the VMDK file to be cloned, as shown in the following image:

```
192.168.1.40 - PuTTY
>
~ #
~ #
~ #
~ # cd /vmfs/volumes/8f3de369-9b8393d4/W7-LC-Base            <===
/vmfs/volumes/8f3de369-9b8393d4/W7-LC-Base # mkdir /vmfs/volumes/8f3de369-9b8393
d4/W7-LC-Base/backup
/vmfs/volumes/8f3de369-9b8393d4/W7-LC-Base # ls
Win 7 Pro-000001-ctk.vmdk        Win 7 Pro.vmdk
Win 7 Pro-000001-delta.vmdk      Win 7 Pro.vmsd
Win 7 Pro-000001.vmdk            Win 7 Pro.vmx
Win 7 Pro-000002-ctk.vmdk        Win 7 Pro.vmx.lck
Win 7 Pro-000002-delta.vmdk      Win 7 Pro.vmxf
Win 7 Pro-000002.vmdk            backup
Win 7 Pro-000003-ctk.vmdk        vmware-25.log
Win 7 Pro-000003-delta.vmdk      vmware-26.log
Win 7 Pro-000003.vmdk            vmware-27.log
Win 7 Pro-325517ed.hlog          vmware-28.log
Win 7 Pro-325517ed.vswp          vmware-29.log
Win 7 Pro-Snapshot16.vmsn        vmware-30.log
Win 7 Pro-ctk.vmdk               vmware.log
Win 7 Pro-flat.vmdk              vmx-Win 7 Pro-844437485-1.vswp
Win 7 Pro.nvram
/vmfs/volumes/8f3de369-9b8393d4/W7-LC-Base #
```

3. Use the vmkfstools command to clone the VMDK file using the command in the following image:

```
vmkfstools -i /vmfs/volumes/8f3de369-9b8393d4/w7-LC-Base/win 7 Pro-000003.vmdk
/vmfs/volumes/8f3de369-9b8393d4/w7-LC-Base/backup/win 7 Pro-000003.vmdk
```

For more information, see *Cloning individual virtual machine disks via the ESX/ESXi host terminal* article, at http://kb.vmware.com/selfservice/microsites/search.do?language=en_US&cmd=displayKC&externalId=1027876.

Once the cloning process is complete, remove the locked disk from the virtual machine using **Remove** from the virtual machine option. Attach the cloned .vmdk file to the virtual machine and power it up.

If this problem persists, contact your backup vendor to determine why the backup server is retaining a lock on the VMDK files after the backup completes.

Unmounting a LUN from ESXi hosts

This section will show you how to unmount a LUN or detach a datastore from multiple VMware ESXi 5.x hosts. The methods discussed here include how to perform this one host at a time and how to accomplish this for multiple hosts at the same time. You will be provided with steps to unmount a LUN from an ESXi 5.x host, which will include unmounting the filesystem along with detaching the device.

The first method is for one host at a time, and the steps must be performed for each of your ESXi hosts.

Note that this is for the 5.x host only. Removing a LUN from an ESXi/ESX 4.x host is very complex. For information on unmounting a datastore in ESXi/ESX 4.x, see Removing a LUN containing a datastore from VMware ESXi 4x and ESX 4.x at http://kb.vmware.com/selfservice/microsites/search.do?language=en_US&cmd=displayKC&externalId=1029786.

Before unmounting a LUN, make sure the following issues are addressed:

- If the LUN in use is used as a VMFS datastore, you need to verify objects such as VMs, snapshots, and any templates stored on that VMFS datastore that are unregistered or moved to a different datastore.

- Any CD/DVD images found on the VMFS datastore also need to be unregistered from the VM.

- The datastore to be unmounted should not be used with the vSphere HA heartbeat.

- The datastore should not be part of a datastore cluster.

- Verify that the datastore is not being managed by a storage **Distributed Resource Scheduler (DRS)**.

- Also check and make sure the datastore was not configured to be used as a partition for diagnostic core dumps.

- Verify that **Storage I/O Control** on the datastore is disabled.

- Verify that the LUN is not being used as a **raw device mapping (RDM)**. If it is, you need to remove the RDM from the VM by clicking on **Edit Settings**, highlighting the RDM hard disk, and clicking on **Remove**. Then, you can select **Delete** from the selected disk or select it if it is not selected. Finally, click on **OK**. Note that this only destroys the mapping file and not the content of the LUN.

- Verify that the LUN/datastore is not being used as the persistent scratch location for the host.

Make sure you obtain the **Network Address Authority Identifier (NAA ID)** of the LUN to be removed, by using the following procedures:

From the vSphere Client, this information is visible in the **Properties** window of the datastore:

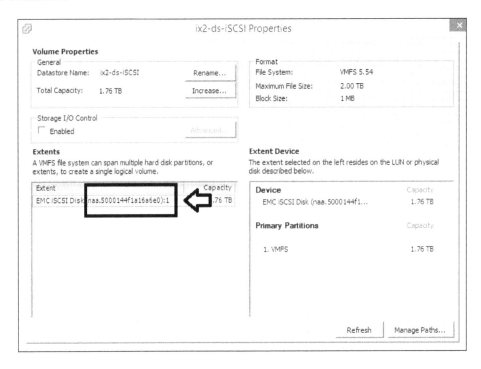

From the ESXi host, run the # `esxcli storage vmfs extent list` command:

Make note of the NAA ID of the datastore to use this information later in this procedure. Alternatively, you can run the `esxcli storage filesystem list` command, which lists all the filesystems recognized by the ESXi host:

Unmounting a LUN using the vSphere Client

To detach a storage device using the vSphere Client, use the **Unmount** command. To unmount a LUN from an ESXi 5.0 host using the vSphere Client in the **Configuration** tab of the ESXi host, click on **Storage**. Right-click on the datastore being removed and then click on **Unmount**:

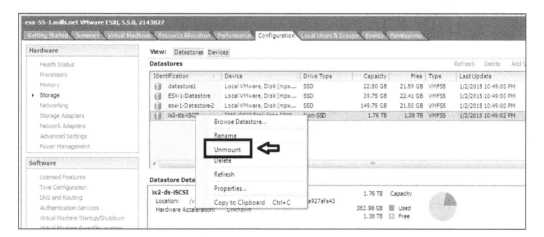

Ensure that the datastore unmount window appears. When the prerequisite criteria have been passed, click on **OK**:

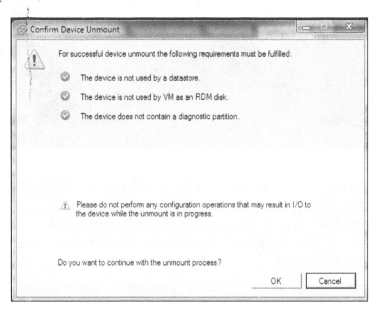

 To unmount a datastore from multiple hosts in the vSphere Client, click on **Hosts** and navigate to **Clusters | Datastores | Datastore Clusters view** (*Ctrl + Shift + D*). Perform the unmount task and select the appropriate hosts that should no longer access the datastore to be unmounted.

You must successfully unmount the datastore using the documented method, prior to completing the detach steps that follow.

Click on the **Devices** option under the **View** tab after you click on **Configuration** and select **Storage** from the pane found on the top pane of the left-hand side of the window. Right-click on the **LUN** option that contains the NAA ID, as noted earlier, and click on **Detach**:

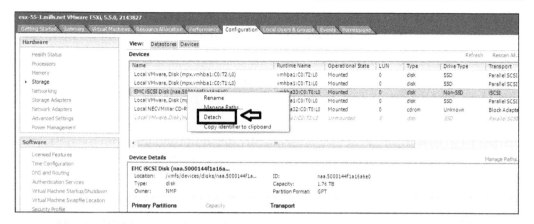

The **Confirm Datastore Unmount** window is displayed. When the prerequisite criteria have been passed, click on **OK**:

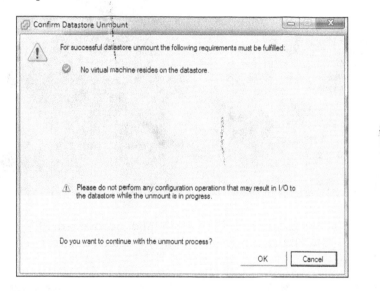

Under the **Operational State of the Device** option, the LUN is listed as Unmounted.

The **Detach** function must be performed on each host and will not propagate the other hosts in vCenter Server. Before unmapping a LUN from the group on the SAN, determine if the LUN is presented to an initiator group or storage group on the SAN. If it is, the **Detach** function must happen on each host in the initiator group. If this is not followed, you will receive an **all-paths-down** (APD) state for those hosts in the storage group for which the **Detach** function was not performed for the LUN that has been selected for the un-mapping.

Confirm that the LUN has been detached successfully. The LUN can then be safely unpresented from the SAN. If you need more information, you should contact your storage array vendor.

Now, perform a rescan on all the ESXi hosts that were associated with the LUN. You should see that the device was automatically removed from the storage adapters.

After the device is detached, it will stay in an unmounted state until the device is reattached. If you want the device permanently decommissioned from the host, you will have to manually remove it. Start by listing the permanently detached devices with the `esxcli storage core device detached list` command:

```
esx-55-1.mills.net - PuTTY
login as: root
Using keyboard-interactive authentication.
Password:
The time and date of this login have been sent to the system logs.

VMware offers supported, powerful system administration tools.  Please
see www.vmware.com/go/sysadmintools for details.

The ESXi Shell can be disabled by an administrative user. See the
vSphere Security documentation for more information.
~ # esxcli storage core device detached list
Device UID            State
--------------------  -----
mpx.vmhba1:C0:T3:L0   off
naa.5000144f1a16a6e0  off
~ #
```

Use the `esxcli storage core device detached remove -d NAA_ID` command and replace `NAA_ID` with the information from the detach device, as shown in the following image:

```
The ESXi Shell can be disabled by an administrative user. See the
vSphere Security documentation for more information.
~ # esxcli storage core device detached list
Device UID            State
--------------------  -----
mpx.vmhba1:C0:T3:L0   off
naa.5000144f1a16a6e0  off
~ # esxcli storage core device detached remove -d naa.5000144f1a16a6e0
~ #
```

Unmounting a LUN using the command line

To unmount a LUN from an ESXi 5.x host using the command line, start with the
`esxcli storage filesystem list` command:

Execute the following command to find the unique identifier of the LUN that has the
datastore to be removed:

This command generates a list of VMFS datastore volumes and the associated unique
identifiers. Be sure to make a note of the unique identifier (`NAA_ID`) for the datastore
to be unmounted. The information will be used later. Next, execute the unmount
command, as shown in the following image:

You can verify that the datastore is unmounted by using the following command. Note that the Mounted field is set to false. The Type field is set to VMFS-unknown version as there is no Mount Point.

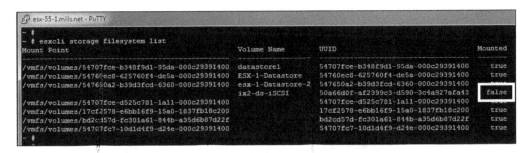

The next step is to detach the device/LUN with the esxcli storage core device set --state=off -d NAA_ID command and verify that the device is offline with esxcli storage core device list -d NAA_ID. Both the commands and the results are shown in the following image. You should replace NAA_ID with the information you collected on the device earlier:

```
esx-55-1.mills.net - PuTTY

~ # esxcli storage core device set --state=off -d naa.5000144f1a16a6e0
~ #
~ #
~ # esxcli storage core device list -d naa.5000144f1a16a6e0
naa.5000144f1a16a6e0
   Display Name: EMC iSCSI Disk (naa.5000144f1a16a6e0)
   Has Settable Display Name: true
   Size: 1843200
   Device Type: Direct-Access
   Multipath Plugin: NMP
   Devfs Path:
   Vendor: EMC
   Model: LIFELINE-DISK
   Revision: 1
   SCSI Level: 4
   Is Pseudo: false
   Status: off
   Is RDM Capable: true
   Is Local: false
   Is Removable: false
   Is SSD: false
   Is Offline: false
   Is Perennially Reserved: false
   Queue Full Sample Size: 0
   Queue Full Threshold: 0
   Thin Provisioning Status: unknown
   Attached Filters:
   VAAI Status: unknown
   Other UIDs: vml.02000000005000144f1a16a6e04c4946454c49
   Is Local SAS Device: false
   Is USB: false
   Is Boot USB Device: false
   No of outstanding IOs with competing worlds: 32
~ #
```

Now, rescan all devices on the host with the `esxcli storage core adapter rescan --all` command. You will find that the devices are automatically removed from the storage adapters. To get a list of the permanently detached devices, use the `esxcli storage core device detached list` command. Both, the commands and the results are shown in the following image:

```
esx-55-1.mills.net - PuTTY
~ #
~ # esxcli storage core adapter rescan
Missing --adapter or --all option
~ # esxcli storage core adapter rescan --all
~ #
~ # esxcli storage core device detached list
Device UID               State
--------------------     -----
naa.5000144f1a16a6e0     off
~ #
~ #
```

You can permanently device configuration information with the command `esxcli storage core device detached remove -d NAA_ID` command. Again, use the `NAA_ID` information collected on the device:

```
esx-55-1.mills.net - PuTTY
~ #
~ #
~ # esxcli storage core device detached remove -d naa.5000144f1a16a6e0
~ #
~ #
~ #
```

Automating datastores detaching with PowerCLI

It is possible to use an automated process to detach the datastores from multiple hosts using PowerCLI scripts. You need to download the PowerCLI script available at *Automating Datastore/Storage Device Detachment in vSphere 5* found at `http://blogs.vmware.com/vsphere/2012/01/automating-datastore-storage-device-detachment-in-vsphere-5.html`.

Please note that the PowerCLI script is provided "as-is" and is supported by the VMware community. Therefore, if you have any issues with this PowerCLI script, you need to seek assistance directly from the VMware Community forums.

After downloading the script, import it using the `Import-Module path_to_script` command.

To list all datastores along with their attached hosts, use the following command:

```
Get-Datastore | Get-DatastoreMountInfo | Sort Datastore, VMHost |
FT -AutoSize
```

Next, select the datastore and make a note of the name found under the `Datastore` column. Confirm that the `Mounted` column contains `False` for all hosts. Then, detach the devices from all hosts by running the following command:

```
Get-Datastore datastore_name| Detach-Datastore
```

Replace the `datastore_name` with the name you recorded earlier.

You see an output similar to the following:

```
Detaching LUN naa.5000123e52345688 from host esx-55-1.local...

Detaching LUN naa. 5000123e52345688 from host esx-55-1.local...

Detaching LUN naa. 5000123e52345688 from host esx-55-1.local...
```

Using vCenter operations for troubleshooting storage devices

The vCenter Operations Management Pack for Storage Devices (Management Pack) can be installed on the vCenter Operations (vCOps) Advanced or Enterprise editions. The installation is designed for both, the appliance and standalone deployments. It will connect to any storage device that has a vStorage APIs for Storage Awareness (VASA) provider. The performance data is collected from the host bus adapter (HBA), VMs, and **Storage Area Network (SAN)** switches.

The Management Pack provides the following benefits:

- Gives you an end-to-end view of the entire data path through the SAN, from the VM, through the Storage Volume

- Provides standardized protocols to storage devices such as CIM, SMI-S, and VASA

- Provides analytics for APD and PDL storage conditions along with dashboards for health and performance

- Captures and analyzes information on throughput and latency for each of your nodes found in the storage path

- Reports on IOps and queue depth on the HBA and the target port for the read/write operations

- Provides aggregate latency at the I/O packet level in the fabric

The VMware Storage Management Pack also provides the following for cloud operations:

- Self-learning analytics that create a higher degree of automation

- An integrated management of performance, capacity, and configuration management

- Includes comprehensive compliance management, application discovery, and monitoring, along with cost metering capabilities

The Management Pack for Storage Devices provides visibility into your storage environment by using common protocols to collect health and performance data from your storage devices. The pack comes with defined dashboards that help to identify and troubleshoot most problems that may exist in the storage environment.

Installing the Management Pack

Verify that you have properly configured the vSphere API for **Storage Awareness** credentials in vCenter. The VASA providers gather information from arrays used to support the environment and then provide the information to vCenter. If you fail to set the credentials before creating the Management Pack instances, the dashboards will display unique identification numbers rather than a readable name for the resources. You can find details on this at `https://pubs.vmware.com/ vsphere-55/index.jsp?topic=%2Fcom.vmware.vsphere.storage.doc%2FGUID-B50E19B8-C1AD-4FE1-AD90-4DD6D29831FE.html&resultof=%22storage%22%20 %22storag%22%20%22provider%22%20%22pr%` or search for *Registered Storage Providers* in the VMware vSphere 5.5 Documentation Center found at `https:// pubs.vmware.com/vsphere-55/index.jsp`.

1. Log in to vCenter Server using the web client and select your vCenter Server.

2. Select the **Manage** tab and then click on **Storage Providers**:

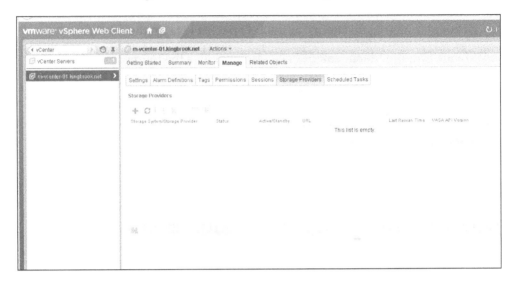

3. Click on the **+** icon to add a new storage provider.

4. Enter the connection information for the storage provider, including the name, URL, and credentials.

5. This step is optional. To direct vCenter Server to the storage provider certificate, select the Use **Storage Provider Certificate** option and then specify the location of the certificate. If this is not selected, a thumbprint of the certificate is displayed. After you check the thumbprint, approve it.

6. Click on **OK** to complete the registration.

Installing the Management Pack in the vCOps vApp

If you have installed vCOps as a vApp, you will install the Management Pack from a PAK file using the following steps:

1. First, you need to download the PAK file from `https://solutionexchange.vmware.com`. If you do not have a Solution Exchange account, you need to create one.

2. Select the **Cloud Management Marketplace** tab.

3. Click on the link for vCenter Operations Management Packs.

4. Use the navigation arrows to locate and click on the link for Management Pack for Storage Devices.

5. Click on the **Try** button to download the installation PAK file.

6. Save the PAK file to a folder.

7. Log in to the admin user interface using the admin account, for example, `https://vCops-ip-address/admin/`:

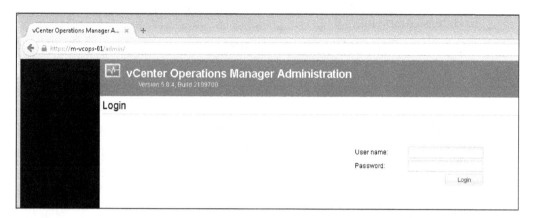

8. After selecting the **Update** tab, click on **Browse** and navigate to the folder where the PAK file is saved:

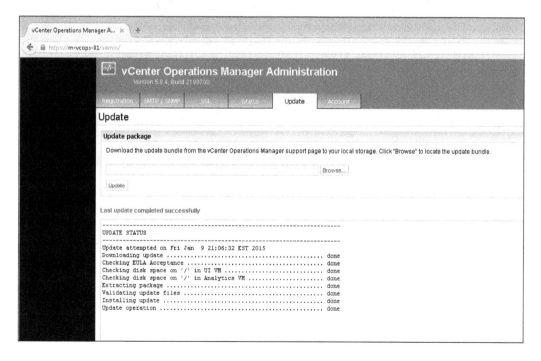

9. Click on **Update** and then click on **OK** to confirm the update. The Admin user interface uploads the PAK file. The upload may take several minutes.

10. Read and accept the **End User License Agreement** (**EULA**) and click on **OK**.

11. Click on **OK** to confirm and start the update process. The update might take several minutes. Status information appears on the **Update** tab when the update is completed.

12. Log in to the **Custom UI** as an administrator, for example `https:// vCops-ip-address /vcops-custom/`:

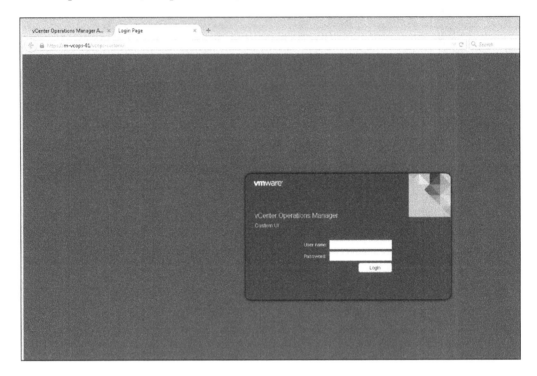

13. Verify that the build number in the `Adapter Version` column for the adapter matches the build number in the `PAK` file that you uploaded.

The Management Pack for **Storage Devices** dashboards are deployed by default when installed on the vCOps vApp.

Installing the Management Pack in the vCOps Standalone Installation

If you have a standalone installation, you will install the Management Pack by extracting the installation files from a TGZ file and perform the installation in the following way:

1. Download the TGZ file at `https://solutionexchange.vmware.com`. If you do not have a Solution Exchange account, you will need to create one.

2. Select the **Cloud Management Marketplace** tab.

3. Choose the vCenter Operations Management Pack for Storage Devices Installation and Configuration Guide.

4. Click on the link for **vCenter Operations Management Packs**.

5. Use the navigation arrows to locate the link for Management Pack for Storage Devices and click on it.

6. Select the **Resources** tab.

7. Click on the link to download the `TGZ` file.

Performing the Management Pack installation procedure

Use the following procedure to install the Management Pack:

1. Open the TGZ file and extract the TAR file to a folder on your vCenter Operations Manager server.

2. In this folder, open the TAR file. Extract and run the installer for the operating system in your environment.

3. Verify that the build number (the `Adapter Version` column for the adapter) is the same as the build number found in the TGZ file you downloaded.

The installer will create the `vcenter-ops/usr/lib/vmwarevcops/user/plugins/inbound/ManagementPackForStorageDevices3` folder and the `ManagementPackForStorageDevices3.jar` file under the `vcenter-ops/usr/lib/vmwarevcops/user/plugins/inbound/` folder.

Installing Management Pack Dashboards in a standalone environment

For a standalone installation, you can import the dashboards manually using a batch file or shell script. In order to do this, you need to navigate to `vcenter-ops/usr/lib/vmwarevcops/user/plugins/inbound/ManagementPackForStorageDevices3/conf/scripts` and execute the appropriate script file depending on your OS.

- For Windows, execute `MPSDPostInstall.bat`
- For Linux, execute `MPSDPostInstall.sh`

Adding a credential to the Management Pack

The Management Pack for Storage Devices will need a username and password in order to connect to the host for vCenter Server. It will also need a username and password for each **Common Information Model** (**CIM**) server that you have in your environment. You can add the credentials before creating the adapter instance and then select the correct credential when defining the adapter instance. Otherwise, you can just add the credential when you define the adapter instance.

To do this, use the following procedure:

1. Log in to the **Custom UI** as an administrator.
2. Navigate to **Environment** | **Configuration** | **Credentials**.
3. Select **Storage Devices** from the **Adapter Kind** drop-down menu.
4. Select **Storage Devices Credential** from the **Credential Kind** drop-down menu.
5. At the top of the list of credentials, next to **Action**, click on **Add**.
6. Type a unique name for the credential instance in the **Instance Name** textbox.
7. Type the username and password for the host for vCenter Server in the **VCUsername** and **VCPassword** textboxes respectively.
8. For each CIM server, type an IP address, username, and password.
9. Click on **OK** to save the credential.

The credential appears in the list in the **Manage Credentials** window.

You can find the complete configuration guide at `https://c368768.ssl.cf1.rackcdn.com/product_files/16274/original/vCenter_Operations_Management_Pack_for_Storage_Devices_Installation_and_Configuration_Guide_V1c63e3d00780ba528eed0a01d6ba3e561.pdf`, or search for the VMware Management Pack for Storage Devices in VMware vSphere 5.5 Documentation Center, found at `https://pubs.vmware.com/vsphere-55/index.jsp` to get details.

Summary

This chapter addressed some of the storage issues faced by administrators. It showed you how to delete virtual machine snapshots that were locked by an application or some other process. It also showed you how to unmount a LUN from multiple ESXi hosts. The chapter concluded by showing you how to install the vCOps Management Pack for Storage Devices. Management Packs are used to monitor and troubleshoot storage devices in the vSphere environment.

The next chapter will review some of the not-so-common vCenter issues, such as fixing problems when your inventory shows no objects. It will also cover how to fix the VPXD error when using the vCenter virtual appliance along with showing the vSphere administrator how to remove the plugins that are no longer needed in the vCenter environment.

6
Solving Some Not-so-common vCenter Issues

This chapter will review some of the not-so-common vCenter issues that administrators could face while they work with the vSphere environment. The chapter will cover the following issues and provide the solutions:

- The vCenter inventory shows no objects after you log in
- You get the **VPXD must be stopped to perform this operation** message
- Removing the vCenter plugins when they are no longer needed

Solving the problem of no objects in vCenter

After successfully completing the vSphere 5.5 installation (not an upgrade) process with no error messages whatsoever, and logging in you log in to vCenter with the account you used for the installation. In this case, it is the local administrator account. Surprisingly, you are presented with an inventory of 0. The first thing is to make sure you have given vCenter enough time to start.

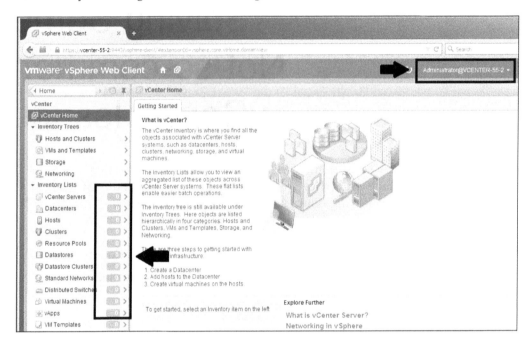

Considering the previously mentioned account was the account used to install vCenter, you would assume the account is granted appropriate rights that allow you to manage your vCenter Server. Also consider the fact that you can log in and receive no objects from vCenter. Then, you might try logging in with your domain administrator account. This makes you wonder, **What is going on here?**

After installing vCenter 5.5 using the Windows option, remember that the `administrator@vsphere.local` user will have administrator privileges for both the *vCenter Single Sign-On Server* and *vCenter Server*. You log in using the `administrator@vsphere.local` account with the password you defined during the installation of the SSO server:

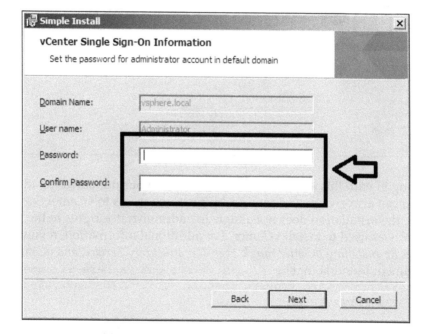

vSphere attaches the permissions along with assigning the role of administrator to the default account `administrator@vsphere.local`. These privileges are given for both the vCenter Single Sign-On server and the vCenter Server system. You must log in with this account after the installation is complete.

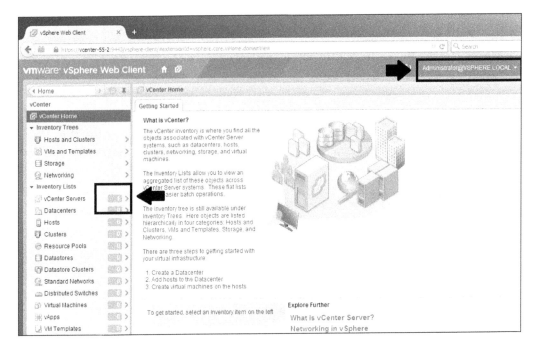

After logging in with this account, you can configure your domain as an identity source. You can also give your domain administrator access to vCenter Server. Remember, the installation does not assign any administrator rights to the user account that was used to install vCenter. For additional information, review the *Prerequisites for Installing vCenter Single Sign-On, Inventory Service, and vCenter Server* document found at `https://pubs.vmware.com/vsphere-51/index.jsp?topic=%2Fcom.vmware.vsphere.install.doc%2FGUID-C6AF2766-1AD0-41FD-B591-75D37DDB281F.html`.

Now that you understand what is going on with the vCenter account, use the following steps to enable the use of your Active Directory account for managing vCenter.

Add or verify your AD domain as an identity source using the following procedure:

1. Log in with `administrator@vsphere.local`.

2. Select **Administration** from the menu.

3. Choose **Configuration** under the **Single Sign-On** option.

You will see the **Single Sign-On | Configuration** option only when you log in using the `administrator@vsphere.local` account.

4. Select the **Identity Sources** tab and verify that the AD domain is listed.

5. If not, choose **Active Directory (Integrated Windows Authentication)** found at the top of the window.

6. Enter your **Domain name** and click on **OK** at the bottom of the window.

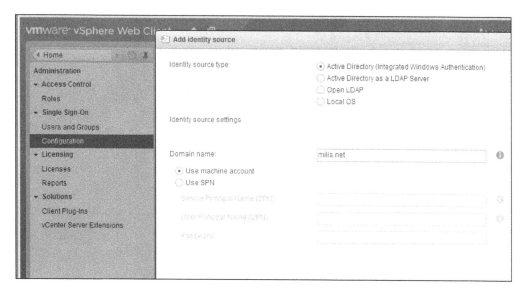

7. Verify that your domain was added to **Identity Sources**, as shown in the following screenshot:

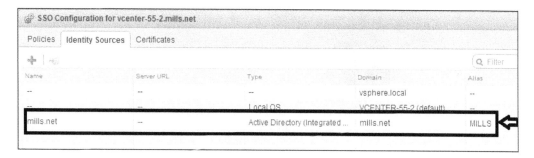

Add the permissions for the AD account using the following steps:

1. Click on **Home** at the top left of the window.

2. Select **vCenter** from the menu options.

3. Select **vCenter Servers** and then choose the vCenter Server object:

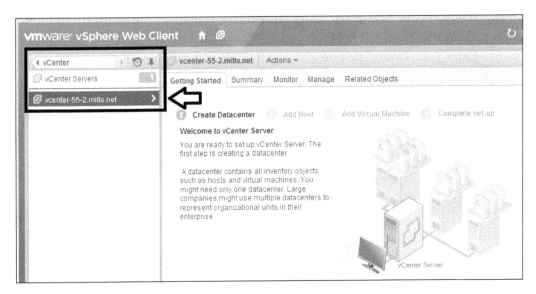

4. Select the **Manage** tab and then the **Permissions** tab found in the vCenter Object window. Review the image that follows the steps to verify the process.

   1. Click on the green **+** icon to add permission.

   2. Choose the **Add** button located at the bottom of the window.

   3. Select the AD domain found in the drop-down option at the top of the window.

   4. Choose a user or group you want to assign permission to (the account named **Chuck** was selected for this example).

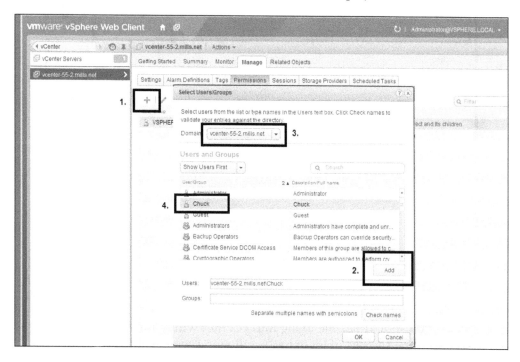

5. Verify that the user or group is selected in the window.

6. Use the drop-down options to choose the level of permissions (verify that **Propagate to children** is checked).

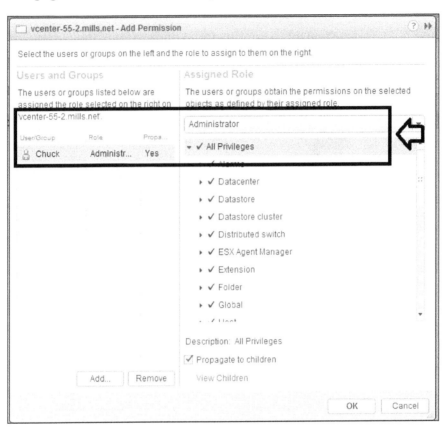

7. Now, you should be able to log into vCenter with your AD account. See the results of the successful login in the following screenshot:

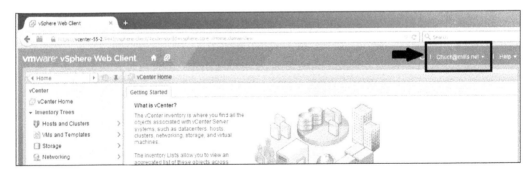

Now, by adding the permissions to the account, you are able to log into vCenter using your AD credentials. The preceding screenshot shows the results of the changes, which is much different than the earlier attempt.

Fixing the VPXD must be stopped to perform this operation message

It has been mentioned several times in this book that the **Virtual Center Service Appliance (VCSA)** is the direction VMware is moving in when it comes to managing vCenter. As the number of administrators using it keeps increasing, the number of problems will also increase. One of the components an administrator might have problems with is the Virtual Centre Server service. This service should not be running during any changes to the database or the account settings. However, as with most vSphere components, there are times when something happens and you need to stop or start a service in order to fix the problem.

There are times when an administrator who works within the VCSA appliance encounters the following error:

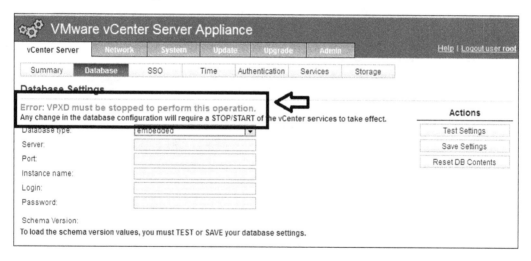

This service can be stopped using the web console, by performing the following steps:

1. Log into the console using `https://ip-of-vcsa:5480`. Enter your username and password:

2. Choose **vCenter Server** after logging in.
3. Make sure the **Summary** tab is selected.
4. Click on the **Stop** button to stop the server:

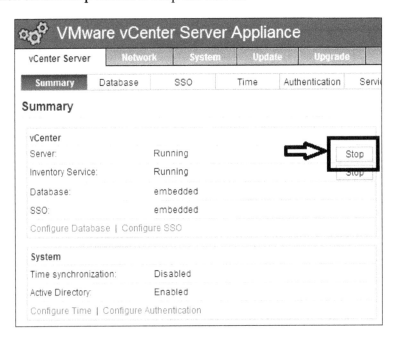

This should work most of the time, but if you find that using the web console is not working, then you need to log into the VCSA appliance directly and use the following procedure to stop the server:

1. Connect to the appliance by using an SSH client such as Putty or mRemote.

2. Type the command `chkconfig`.

3. This will list all the services and their current status:

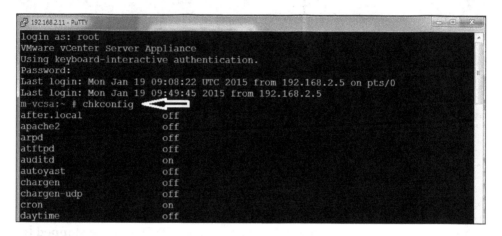

4. Verify that `vmware-vxpd` is on:

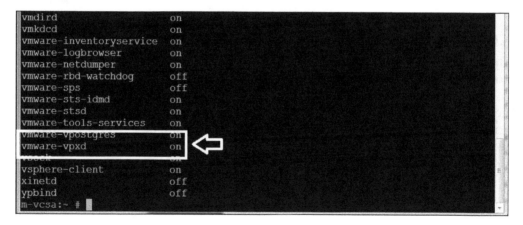

5. You can stop the server by using `service vmware-vpxd stop` command:

```
vmware-tools-services     on
vmware-vpostgres          on
vmware-vpxd               on
vsock                     on
vsphere-client            on
xinetd                    off
ypbind                    off
m-vcsa:~ # service vmware-vpxd stop      <=
Stopping VMware vSphere Profile-Driven Storage Service...
Stopped VMware vSphere Profile-Driven Storage Service.
Stopping tomcat: success
Stopping vmware-vpxd: success
Shutting down ldap-server..done
```

After completing your work, you can start the server using one of the following methods:

- Restart the VCSA appliance
- Use the web console by clicking on the **Start** button on the vCenter Summary page
- Type `service vmware-vpxd start` on the SSH command line

This should fix the issues that occur when you see the **VPXD must be stopped to perform this operation** message.

Removing unwanted plugins in vSphere

Administrators add and remove tools from their environment based on the needs and also the life of the tool. This is no different for the vSphere environment. As the needs of the administrator change, so does the usage of the plugins used in vSphere. The following section can be used to remove any unwanted plugins from your current vCenter. So, if you have lots of plugins and they are no longer needed, use the follow procedure to remove them:

1. Log into your vCenter using `http://vCenter_name` or `IP_address/mob` and enter your username and password:

2. Click on the **content** link under Properties:

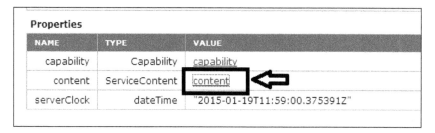

3. Click on **ExtensionManager**, which is found in the **VALUE** column:

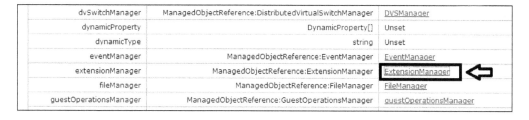

4. Highlight, right-click, and **Copy** the extension to be removed.

 Check out the Knowledge Base 1025360 found at http:// Kb.vmware. com/kb/1025360 to get an overview of the plugins and their names.

5. Select **UnregisterExtension** near the bottom of the page:

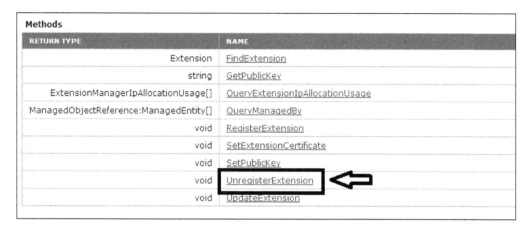

RETURN TYPE	NAME
Extension	FindExtension
string	GetPublicKey
ExtensionManagerIpAllocationUsage[]	QueryExtensionIpAllocationUsage
ManagedObjectReference:ManagedEntity[]	QueryManagedBy
void	RegisterExtension
void	SetExtensionCertificate
void	SetPublicKey
void	UnregisterExtension
void	UpdateExtension

6. Right-click on the plugin name and **Paste** it into the Value field:

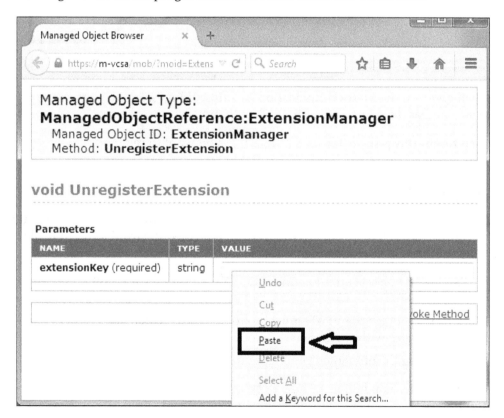

7. Click on **Invoke Method** to remove the plugin:

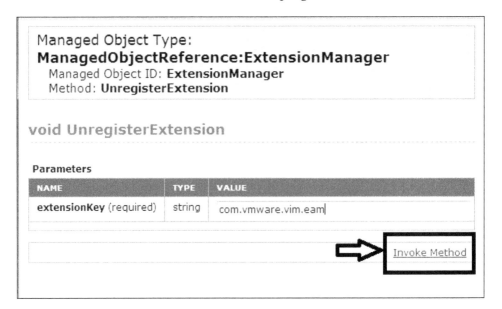

This will give you the **Method Invocation Result: void** message. This message informs you that the selected plugin has been removed.

You can repeat this process for each plugin that you want to remove.

Summary

In this chapter, we covered some of the not-so-common challenges an administrator could encounter in the vSphere environment. It provided the troubleshooting along with the solutions to the following issues:

- Seeing NO objects after logging into vCenter with the account you used to install it
- How to get past the VPXD must be stopped error when you are performing certain tasks within vCenter
- Removing the unwanted plugins from vCenter Server

In the next chapter you will learn how to be prepared for every administrator's nightmare, recovering a vSphere environment. We provide guidance on how to protect the investment made in putting together your vCenter solution. We also learnt what you need to backup, and the process to perform the backup, which is just as important as the recovery process.

7
Backup and Recovery

There is nothing that worries an administrator more than losing data or components of their infrastructure. In order to prevent this from happening in the vSphere environment, you should always perform backups of the system, so, if for some reason there is a major problem or corruption, you have a method to recover. The first step toward protecting your vCenter is to have a good backup of the important components.

These procedures should be developed and tested before the disaster happens. There is nothing like trying to figure out how to recover from a problem when you don't have a recent backup or you do not have the exact process to perform the restore. Having a clearly documented backup and recovery procedure will allow the administrator to focus on the actual recovery, and not on wondering how to approach the problem.

Now that you have the backup and recovery procedure, as mentioned earlier, you can use it to protect your infrastructure from unexpected problems. Each vSphere is different and adjustment will be needed based on the composition of your environment. Note that the information presented here is based on the Windows version of vCenter. Backup/recovery should be scheduled based on the frequency of changes in the environment, along with how much data loss a company is willing to tolerate.

Your backup and recovery solution should be based on two factors: **Recovery Time Objective (RTO)** and **Recovery Point Objective (RPO)**. RTO is the targeted amount of time from which the environment must be restored after a declared disaster and RPO is the maximum selected period from when the data might be lost. For example, we cannot lose more than 8 hours of work (RPO) and we must be working again in 36 hours (RTO). Use these factors to develop a backup and recovery plan that supports the company's requirements.

Special backups should be performed when changes are going to happen to the environment, such as but not limited to:

- After you complete an install, update, or change to the vCenter SSO instance, including a location change

- Before you are planning a restore from a snapshot of the vCenter Server VM

- Before any major changes to the database, including a restore from a prior instance of the vCenter Server

Procedure for backing up vCenter SSO 5.5

The vCenter **Single Sign On** (**SSO**) is a very critical part of the vSphere environment that allows all of the different components to use a secure token exchange process to communicate with each other. If your vCenter SSO fails or is corrupted, then all vCenter Servers, along with the Inventory Service and vSphere Web Client instances associated with that SSO, will lose access to vSphere. This means you must have a backup of this component. A good backup of the SSO should be made and unless there are major changes made, you should not need a scheduled backup.

This procedure is a manual process to back up the vCenter SSO configuration for 5.5. This procedure includes steps that modify the Windows registry. This means you should have a current backup of the registry, along with the vCenter VM. The steps for the backup procedure are as follows:

1. Generate the log bundle from the vCenter SSO by logging into the vCenter server and navigating to **Start** | **All Programs** | **VMware**.

2. Right-click on **Generate vCenter Single Sign-On log bundle** and choose **Run as administrator**.

3. This will generate a log bundle and place the folder on the desktop of the current user. You can also execute the following from a Command Prompt opened as an administrator:

```
cscript "C:\Program Files\VMware\Infrastructure\VMware\cis\
vmware-sso\vm-support\sso-support.wsf"
```

The following screenshot shows the Command Prompt after executing the preceding command:

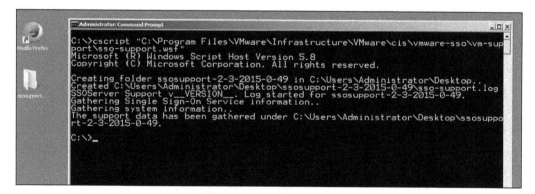

Creating a backup of Windows registry keys

You can create a backup of Windows registry keys using the following steps:

1. Navigate to **Start | Run**, type regedit, and press *Enter*. The **Registry Editor** window will open.

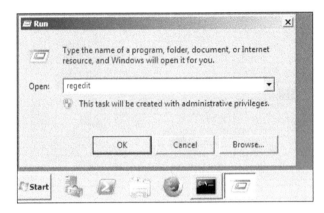

2. Export the following registry folder:

   HKEY_LOCAL_MACHINE\SYSTEM\CurrentControlSet\services\
   VmwareDirectoryService

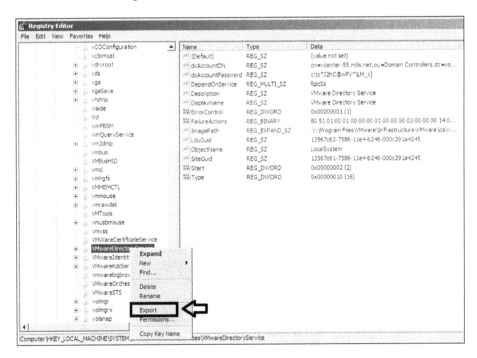

3. Create a backup of SSL certificates, the KDC data folder, and the certificate server data by saving the folder and contents in the following locations:

  ° For the SSL certificates use C:\ProgramData\VMware\CIS\runtime\VMwareSTS\conf

The following image shows the summary of the backup created:

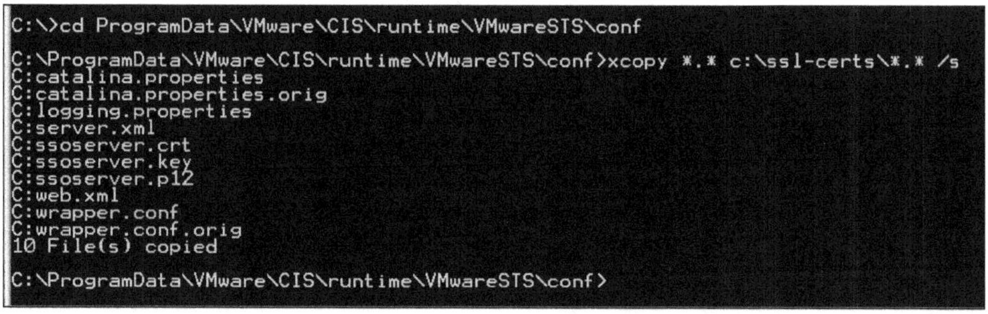

```
C:\>cd ProgramData\VMware\CIS\runtime\VMwareSTS\conf

C:\ProgramData\VMware\CIS\runtime\VMwareSTS\conf>xcopy *.* c:\ssl-certs\*.* /s
C:catalina.properties
C:catalina.properties.orig
C:logging.properties
C:server.xml
C:ssoserver.crt
C:ssoserver.key
C:ssoserver.p12
C:web.xml
C:wrapper.conf
C:wrapper.conf.orig
10 File(s) copied

C:\ProgramData\VMware\CIS\runtime\VMwareSTS\conf>
```

  ° For the certificate server data, use C:\ProgramData\VMware\CIS\data\vmca and its contents.

  ° For the KDC data, use C:\ProgramData\VMware\CIS\cfg\vmkdcd and C:\ProgramData\MIT\Kerberos5

Creating a backup of the VMware Inventory Service Database

The vCenter Inventory Service Database contains information on the **Storage Management Service** and **Profile-Driven Storage Service** and by default, is found at C:\Program Files\VMware\Infrastructure. Use the following steps to create a backup:

1. Open a Command Prompt.

2. Create a new directory that will be used to store the backup of the database. For example, use the following command:

   mkdir C:\MDBBackup

3. Then use the following command to change to the following directory:

   cd C:\Program Files\VMware\Infrastructure\VMware\CIS\vmdird

4. Execute the following command to backup the database:

```
vdcbackup C:\ProgramData\VMware\cis\data\vmdird C:\MDBBackup
```

The following screenshot shows the Command Prompt after executing the preceding command:

This will create a copy of the `data.mdb` and `lock.mdb` files and will put them in the `C:\MDBBackup` area that you created. The following screenshot shows the summary of the copied files to the `C:\MDBBackup` area:

Make sure you protect the `MDBBackup` folder using your standard backup procedures.

Restoring the vCenter SSO 5.5 configuration

The following sections will show you how to restore vCenter for two different scenarios:

- From a full operating system-level backup
- From a vCenter 5.5 database backup

Restoring from a vCenter SSO 5.5 full operating system-level backup

This procedure is based on the recovery of an existing vCenter Server that is running in the environment but has become unusable. You must have an OS-Level backup of the vCenter Server. You will shut down the current unusable vCenter server and restore it from your backup. After the vCenter backup is restored and running, your recovery steps are as follows:

1. Stop the SSO services on the restored version of the vCenter Server system in this order:
   - **VMware Secure Token Service**
   - **VMware Identity Management Service**
   - **VMware Certificate Service**
   - **VMware KDC Service**
   - **VMware Directory Service**

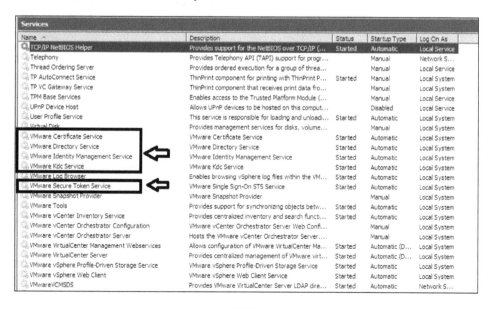

2. To restore the VMware Directory Service (VMdir) database, you need to stop the service as shown in the preceding screenshot and go to the VMdir directory with the following command:

   `cd C:\ProgramData\VMware\cis\data\vmdird`

3. Then, copy the `data.mdb` and `lock.mdb` files from the backup folder to the VMdir directory.

4. Change to the folder that contains `vmdir.exe` by using the following command:

   `cd C:\Program Files\VMware\Infrastructure\VMware\CIS\vmdird`

5. Begin the restore process with the following command:

   `vmdird.exe -c -m restore`

   The following screenshot shows the Command Prompt after executing the preceding command:

This will start the **VMware Directory Service** (**VMdir**) in restore mode and the process ends when the restore is complete.

- After the restore mode process has completed successfully, start the SSO services on your newly restored vCenter Server in the following order:

    ◦ VMware Directory Service
    ◦ VMware Kdc Service
    ◦ VMware Certificate Service
    ◦ VMware Identity Management Service
    ◦ VMware Secure Token Service

  The following screenshot shows the **VMware Directory Service Properties** (**VCENTER-55**) window:

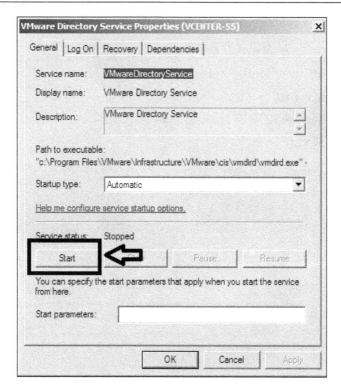

Restoring from a vCenter 5.5 database backup

This procedure is based on the assumption that you need to build a new Windows host system and then manually restore a vCenter SSO from a database backup. You begin the process by creating the host machine to be used to restore the vCenter SSO instance. Make sure you name the new host machine with the same name as your failed SSO instance.

 This procedure is going to modify the Windows registry, and you should perform a backup of the registry before making any changes.

To restore vCenter from your database backup, perform the following steps:

1. You need to install SSO 5.5 on the new host machine as described earlier.

2. Stop the SSO services on the new vCenter Server in the following order:

   ○ VMware Secure Token Service
   ○ VMware Identity Management Service
   ○ VMware Certificate Service
   ○ VMware KDC Service
   ○ VMware Directory Service

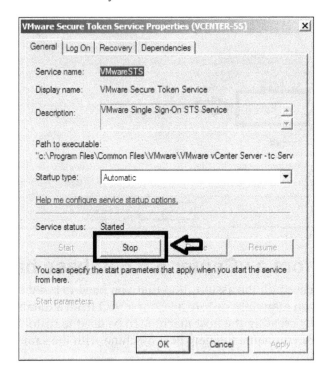

Restore the **VMware Directory Service** registry folder using the following steps:

1. Navigate to **Start | Run**, type `regedit`, and press *Enter*.

2. After opening the **Registry Editor**, navigate to **File | Import** and select the **Backup key**.

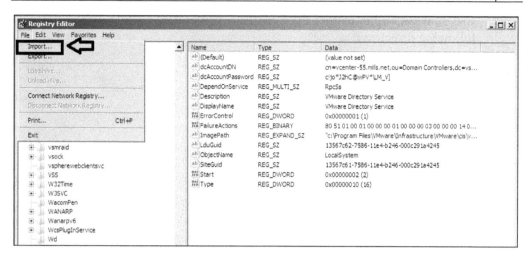

3. Choose the backup file that you used to back up the registry entry.

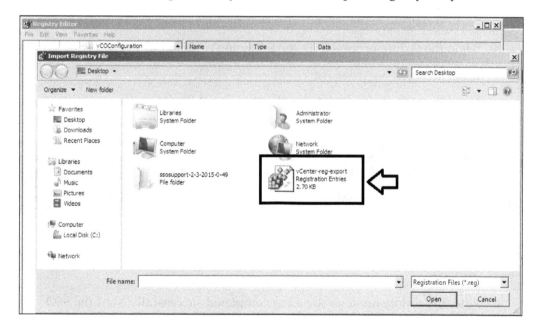

4. Restore the SSL certificates using the backup copy of the conf folder you saved and place the contents in the following directory:

```
C:\ProgramData\VMware\CIS\runtime\VMwareSTS\conf
```

5. Use your backup to restore the Certificate server data to the following directory:

    ```
    C:\ProgramData\VMware\CIS\data\vmca
    ```

6. Restore the KDC data using your backup of these directories:

    ```
    C:\ProgramData\VMware\CIS\cfg\vmkdcd
    ```

    ```
    C:\ProgramData\MIT\Kerberos5
    ```

7. Then, restore the **VMware Directory Service** (**VMdir**) database. Now, stop the service as we did earlier. Go to the VMdir directory with the following code:

    ```
    cd C:\ProgramData\VMware\cis\data\vmdird
    ```

8. Then, copy the `data.mdb` and `lock.mdb` files from the backup folder to the VMdir directory.

9. Change to the folder that contains `vmdir.exe` using the following command:

    ```
    cd C:\Program Files\VMware\Infrastructure\VMware\CIS\vmdird
    ```

10. Begin the restore process with the following command:

    ```
    vmdird.exe -c -m restore
    ```

    The following screenshot shows the Command Prompt after executing the preceding command:

This will start the `VMdir` database in restore mode and the process ends when the restore is completed. Once the restore is completed use the following process to start the SSO services:

1. After the restore mode process has completed successfully, start the SSO services on your newly restored vCenter Server in the following order:
    - VMware Directory Service
    - VMware KDC Service
    - VMware Certificate Service
    - VMware Identity Management Service
    - VMware Secure Token Service

The following screenshot shows the **VMware Directory Service Properties (VCENTER-55)** window:

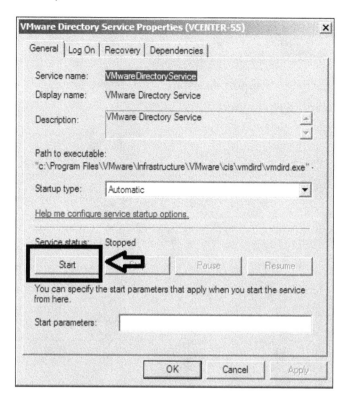

2. Continue with the installation of vSphere 5.5 to complete the restore of the vCenter Server.

Summary

In this chapter, we showed you how to recover when something happens to the vSphere environment. As mentioned in the beginning of this chapter, the first step to protecting your vCenter is to have a good backup of the important components. This chapter provided the items and commands needed to perform the backups if something happens that requires a complete recovery of the vCenter.

Then, if there comes a time when recovery is needed, the chapter explains the commands needed and the order these commands should be executed in. This should give the administrator the confidence needed to not only protect the vCenter server, but the steps to perform a recovery in a timely fashion.

The next chapter shows the administrator how to use the vCenter Support Assistant to obtain quicker responses to reported problems. When there are problems in your environment, you want to get the answers as fast as possible. The chapter also explores some of the free tools used to support the vSphere environment.

The next chapter will cover the following topics:

- Using the vCenter Support Assistant
- Free VMware vSphere tools

8
Additional Support Methods and Tools

This chapter will focus on the tools you can use to monitor and troubleshoot your vSphere environment. The good news is that most of the tools listed in this chapter are free. The chapter will start with the **VMware vCenter Support Assistant**, which is a free solution from VMware that collects data from your environment and can package information to be submitted with a support request. The next section will introduce you to **VMware Labs Flings**. Flings are tools written by VMware engineers in their spare time and are normally targeted for a specific need. They are definitely worth looking at. The final section will highlight free tools that have evolved in the VMware community, along with websites that have some of the most comprehensive list of free tools that I have come across.

VMware vCenter Support Assistant

The VMware vCenter Support Assistant is used to collect diagnostic data on your vSphere environment. It is a free tool from VMware and is used to alert you of problems in your environment so that you can take action before they become bigger problems.

The Support Assistant performs the following functions:

- Problems discovered by the vCenter Support Assistant will be reported to the vSphere Client as alarms. It sends proactive alerts along with recommended fixes. The notifications within vCenter Server will help you become aware of problems and then accordingly recommend solutions.

- Allows the transmission of selected support bundles automatically by configuring the Assistant to collect support bundles selected by you and then transmits them to VMware Technical Support on a regular basis. The information will be matched against a list of known problems.

- Provides the configuration of data collection times by allowing you to select the files, the collection frequency, and then the transmission time. You can use this to minimize the impact on the performance of your system.

- Sends monthly e-mails that summarize the status of problems, which allows you to track problems over time.

- Allows the collection of diagnostic information and attaches that information to support requests. This generates support bundles and then automatically attaches them to a support request along with other files.

- Gives you the ability to view the existing support requests, which includes the status of your existing request. You can add comments for the VMware Technical Support team, view the e-mail exchanges, and also upload any additional diagnostic data or other information regarding your support request.

Requirements for the vCenter Support Assistant

The hardware and networking requirements needed to install the vCenter Support Assistant are discussed in the upcoming subsections.

Hardware

You can install the **vCenter Support Assistant**, which is distributed as a virtual appliance, on systems that meet the minimum hardware requirements. These requirements are found in Table 2-1 of the *Installing and Configuring vCenter Support Assistant*, available at `http://www.vmware.com/pdf/vc-support-assistant-55-install-config.pdf`.

The following image shows the Table 2-1 of the *Installing and Configuring vCenter Support Assistant*:

Number of vCPUs	2
vRAM	2GB
Disk space	Minimum 65gb. Disk space is calculated by the equation: Disk space = 50GB + (number of vCenter servers * 300MB + number of ESXihosts) * 50MB

Networking

The networking requirements found in Table 2-2 of *Installing and Configuring vCenter Support Assistant* are shown in the following screenshot:

Internal Connections

Machine	Connection To	Connection Type	Port
vSphere Web Client	vCenter Support Assistant appliance	Local network connection	8443
vCenter Support Assistant appliance	vCenter Server and ESX/ESXi hosts that you want to collect support data from	Local network connection	

External Connections

Machine	Connection To	Connection Type	Port
vCenter Support Assistant appliance	https://vmware.com	Internet connection	443
	https://supportassistant.vmware.com/*	Internet connection	443
	vcsa.vmware.com/*	Internet connection	443
	ftpsite.vmware.com	Internet connection	21
	vmware.com	Internet connection	80
	ftpsite.vmware.com/*	Internet connection	443
	https://phtransfer.vmware.com/*	Internet connection	443

Installing and configuring the vCenter Support Assistant

The vCenter Support Assistant is found on the VMware website. A search on the site will lead you to the download. After the download is complete, use the following steps to perform the installation.

1. Log in to the vSphere Web Client using an administrator account.

2. In the vSphere Web Client, select an inventory object that is the parent object of a VM (datacenter, folder, cluster, resource pool, or host).

3. Navigate to **Actions | Deploy OVF Template**.

4. Browse to the downloaded OVA file and click on **Next**.

5. Review the **OVF** details and click on **Next**.

6. Click on **Accept** after reading the EULA and click on **Next**.

7. Accept the name and folder, or type in a name selection, and choose the folder for deployment.

8. Choose the datacenter for the deployment and click on **Next**.

9. Choose the virtual disk format and VM Storage Policy. Following information box will give you an explanation of the different virtual disk format types.

- **Thick Provisioned Lazy Zeroed**: This creates a virtual disk in the default thick format. The space required for the virtual disk is allocated at the time the virtual disk is created. Any data remaining on the physical device will not be erased during the creation, but will be zeroed out at a later time (on demand) during the first write issued from the VM.
- **Thick Provision Eager Zeroed**: This is a type of thick virtual disk that will support clustering features, such as fault tolerance. The space required for the virtual disk will be allocated at the time of creation. The data remaining on the physical device will be zeroed out during the creation of the virtual disk. The format time for this option takes much longer than needed for other types of disk.
- **Thin Provision**: This format is used to save storage space. Thin disk uses only as much datastore space as the disk needs for its initial operations and will grow as needed to the total disk space entered.

10. Choose the datastore to store the OVF template in and click on **Next**.

11. For the setup networks, select the destination network to be used. The Source column shows the networks defined in the OVF template and the Destination column shows the target networks. Select the IP protocol and click on **Next**.

12. Enter the **Networking Properties** for the OVF template based on your needs.

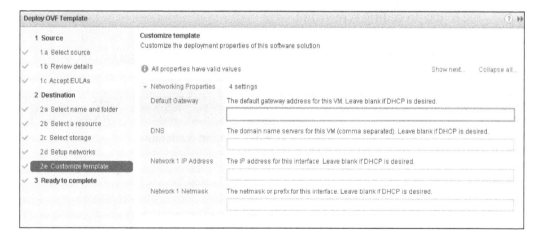

13. Verify your settings and select **Power on after deployment**.

14. Click on **Finish** to complete the deployment.

    After the appliance has completed the install and powered on, you can open the console window to verify and obtain the IP address of the appliance.

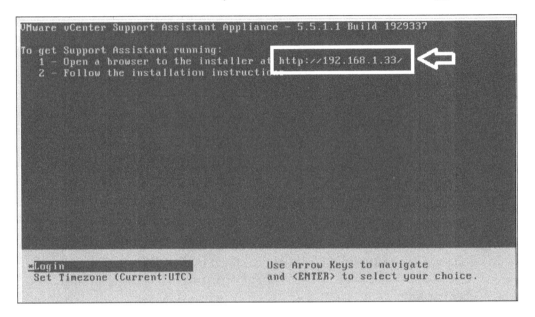

15. Open a Web browser and enter the IP address of the appliance, as you can see in the preceding screenshot.

16. You can log in to the Support Assistant appliance using the default username root with the default password vmware. You should change this password after you have logged in.

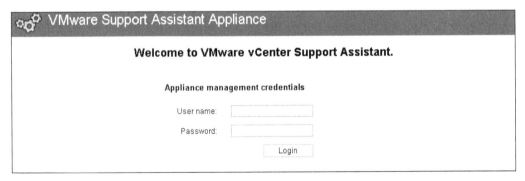

17. Tick that you understood the privacy terms and conditions, and then click on **Next**.

18. The next step is to establish a connection to the lookup service server and then enter the SSO IP address or FQDN in the **Lookup Service Address** box.

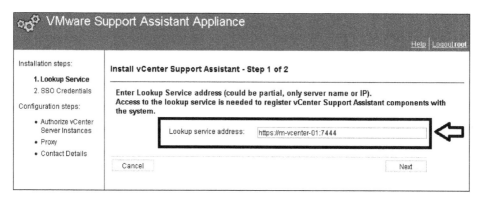

19. Click on **Next** to accept the SSOs SSL certificate.

To connect to vCenter Server, the vCenter Single Sign-On credentials are needed. The Support Assistant has a solution user that is used to retrieve support information from vCenter Server. In order to create the Support Assistant Single Sign-On solution user, you provide the vCenter Single Sign-On administrative credentials. This will register the vCenter Single Sign-On solution user account for the Support Assistant in the vCenter Single Sign-On.

20. Now, enter the **User name** and **Password** (this is the password created during the setup of vCenter) of the vCenter SSO (which is `administrator@vsphere.local` in most of the cases).

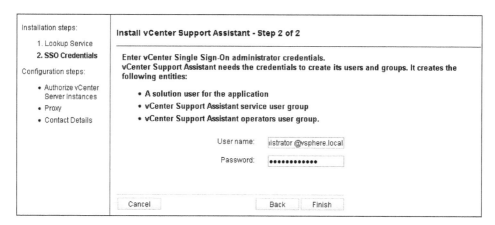

Now we will configure the Support Assistant to collect information and receive alerts from selected vCenter Server instances. You will authorize the Support Assistant so that it can work with the vCenter Server instances for the following:

- ° Generating support bundles
- ° Creating and deleting alarms
- ° Triggering alarms
- ° Obtaining licensing information
- ° Querying ESXi network information, like IP addresses

21. At the **Default administrator user name** and **Default administrator user password**, input the username and password for the vCenter Server administrator. A dedicated account would be the best practice.

22. Click on **Disable strict certificate checks** if you are using self-signed SSL certificates with your vCenter.

23. Click on your vCenter and input the administrator username and password where indicated.

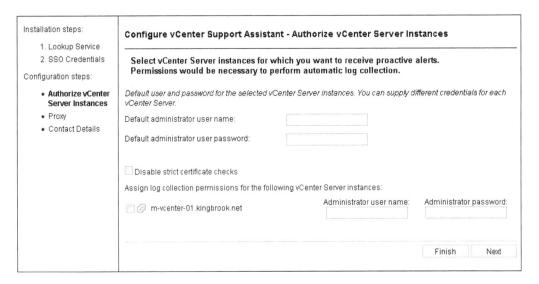

24. Click on **Next** if you do not need to configure proxy settings.

If the connection uses a company firewall, you can configure the Support Assistant to use a proxy to access the Internet. The proxy is disabled by default. Enable the **Use proxy server** checkbox and input the information about your proxy settings. Click on **Test Connectivity** to verify your connection through the proxy server. And then, click on **Next**.

25. You can provide an e-mail address to have notifications and reports sent on behalf of the Support Assistant. This is optional.

After you complete the configuration for **vCenter Support Assistant Appliance**, you will see the **Configuration** section in the **Overview** tab. Click on **Test connectivity**, found under the **Miscellaneous** section. If all the information was entered correctly, you will get a result saying **Connectivity is OK**.

Change the hostname or the certificate of this appliance under **VA Settings**.

The following screenshot shows the information from the **Support Assistant** configured in your vCenter server:

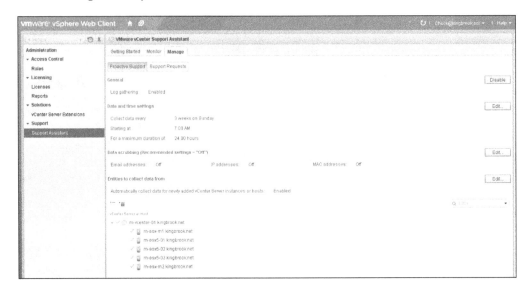

The data scrubbing option

You can select the type of data to obscure in the log files, such as e-mail addresses, IP addresses, and MAC addresses. Not sending the data can affect the content and accuracy of the alerts generated by the vCenter Support Assistant. This omission of data can cause delays in the VMware Technical Support response time. Choosing to scrub data also presents a performance impact on the support collection process due to the number of I/O operations it generates. Make sure you understand and comply with your company's processes when answering this option.

You can use this page to make any modification to items, such as the date and time setting for collecting the information, along with the vCenter and/or Host information.

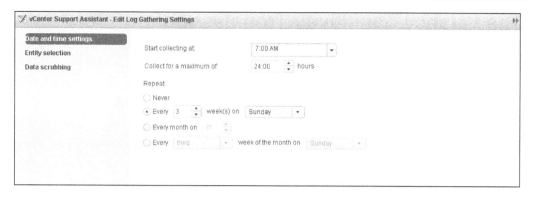

You now have the appliance installed and configured. Review the *vCenter Support Assistant User's Guide* for more information on creating support requests, found at `https://www.vmware.com/pdf/vc-support-assistant-55-users-guide.pdf`.

VMware Labs Flings

Flings are normally created by VMware engineers who address a specific challenge and is not a utility that is found in the VMware product. It is possible that some Flings can be developed into official products. The need is driven when engineering team is working on a product or project that needs additional information and there is not a utility to give them what they are looking for. Many developers create these types of utility solutions and then find them useful on other projects. After the Flings are made available, the user community can provide feedback and request additional features to be incorporated into the current version. There have been times when VMware has queried the user community to submit their ideas for other useful software tools in the Open Innovation Contest. This gives the VMware technology teams the opportunity to develop some of the ideas into a VMware Fling.

There is a stern warning for any of the Flings. The website states that Flings are experimental and should not be run on production systems. Any Fling you plan to use should be evaluated in a test/development environment before they are used in your live environment. There is a lot of community information available regarding Flings and you should research the Fling you are interested in to make sure there are no known problems.

The entire Fling inventory can be found at `https://labs.vmware.com/flings`.

The upcoming sections are a few Flings that can help you with your vSphere environment.

The Latency Sensitivity Troubleshooting Tool

This Fling provides scripts along with examples to troubleshoot configuration and performance problems with the Latency Sensitivity feature in version 5.5 of vSphere.

The VM Resource and Availability Service

This Fling allows you to perform what-if analysis around host failures in your infrastructure. It allows you to simulate a failure on one or more hosts within a cluster (in vSphere) to identify:

- The number of VMs that would be safely restarted on different hosts
- The number of VMs that would fail to be restarted
- The number of VMs that would experience performance degradation after they are restarted on a different host

This will allow you to better plan the placement and configuration of your VM within the environment to reduce downtime when you experience a host failure.

The I/O Analyzer

The VMware I/O Analyzer Fling is a framework designed to measure storage performance within the virtual environment and assist in diagnosing storage performance issues. It is a virtual appliance and automates the storage performance analysis through a unified interface. The interface can configure and deploy storage tests and provides graphical results for the tests.

InventorySnapshot

InventorySnapshot allows a user to back up (snapshot) a selected vCenter inventory configuration and then reproduce it. The datacenter folders, datacenters, clusters, resource pools, vApps, hierarchy, roles and permissions, configuration settings, and custom fields are all included in the snapshot. This means an inventory with a set of hosts and VMs that is organized into clusters can be reproduced, including the administrator-defined cluster settings and custom roles.

This can be helpful if you have spent a lot of time creating a vCenter development environment and you want to move it into production. The Fling snapshots your developed environment and it can then be deployed to production. The Fling also comes with the documentation.

Finding resources to support your VMware environment

A search for free VMware tools will result in over 17 million results. This involves a lot of time searching for what you need. The VMware community provides websites that collect the many of the URLs and aggregates them into portal of sorts.

Here are a few sites that will help you if you are looking for tools (mostly free) to support your vSphere environment:

- *101 Free Tools for VMware Administrators* can be found at `http://www.vmwarearena.com/2013/06/101-free-tools-for-vmware-administrators.html`

- *A List of FREE VMware vSphere Tools* can be found at `http://kendrickcoleman.com/index.php/Tech-Blog/a-list-of-free-vmware-vsphere-tools.html`

- *TechHead VMware Tools* can be found at `http://techhead.co/vmware-esx-tools/`

Some of the tools here are for non-vSphere (Horizon View) installs, but there are more than enough vSphere solutions.

Summary

This chapter gave the information needed to find and select tools you can use to monitor and troubleshoot your vSphere environment. The first tool was the VMware vCenter Support Assistant, which is a free solution from VMware. This tool collects data from your environment and also allows you to package diagnosis information that can be submitted with a support request. The chapter introduced VMware Labs Flings in *VMware Labs Flings* section and what they are and how they can be used. The final section provides a few websites that have collected URLs from the Internet and has created a single site to research and obtain vSphere tools. Most of these tools are free, which helps with the IT budget.

The next chapter will cover how to approach problems with a standard method that helps you discover the cause of many of those problems and allows you to correct them on your own. The chapter will cover the following:

- How to verify the behavior is not what you want
- Then, isolating the behavior of the problem
- Identifying the factors
- Finally, determining the correct support steps

This will help administrators make sure their problems are identified and corrected quickly or at least assure them that there is a plan in place to solve the problems and keep their vSphere environment healthy.

Troubleshooting Methods

9

Any administrator's aim is to keep the vSphere environment in top working order, but there will be problems that occur from time to time. When this happens, the administrator needs to have a plan to find the problem, determine the impact on the environment and quickly come up with a resolution. This chapter will give guidance on developing a troubleshooting plan, and provide the information needed to decide on fixing the issue or opening a support ticket with the vendor, or other support solutions.

Troubleshooting workflow

Troubleshooting an issue should follow a workflow process that allows you to discover the cause of problems and then help you decide whether you can fix them on your own, or allow you to gather the information needed by a technical support team that can give you further assistance.

This chapter will not review all the methodologies or try to choose one that is better, but will stress the use of a methodology that helps to put a repeatable process around finding and solving problems in your vSphere environment. This process can be used for most areas of the IT infrastructure, and can also be used to provide any technical support services provided by the vendor or other third-party companies with the information needed to solve the problem.

The following diagram gives an example of a troubleshooting workflow. A description of each component of the workflow will be provided in this chapter.

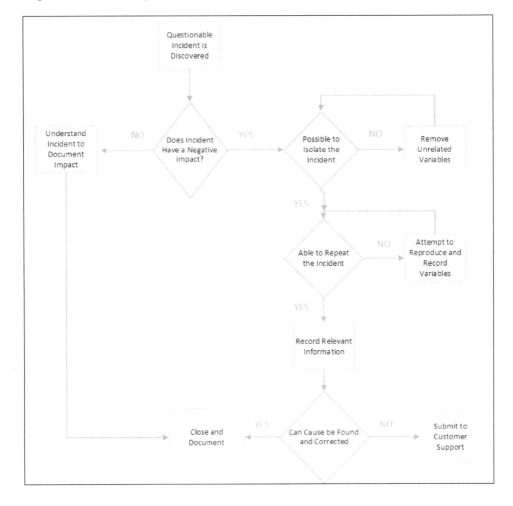

The preceding diagram shows an example of a troubleshooting flow. There are two types of boxes in the diagram. The diamond-shaped boxes are decisions and ask a question. The answer will lead the process to another box. Most answers should be framed with a **YES** or **NO**. The square boxes are actions that should be completed in the flow, and after they are finished you should move to the next box.

This is just an example of the flow the author would use when trying to resolve an issue in the environment. You can use this as it is or modify it to create a method that would work for you, or follow an established business practice used by your company.

Each of the upcoming sections will have information on each of the boxes in the preceding diagram. As you read each section, think whether it's a decision point or a section that requires processing.

A questionable incident is discovered

Questionable incidents can be described as an event that happens where the result is different from what you expected. This can come from a number of sources.

- Is this a feature you normally do not use, and so maybe you are not familiar with the results?

- Is the feature named something, but the result does not match the description?

- Is this a new event or feature that appeared after an upgrade or update?

In any case, you have a situation that needs to be investigated so as to determine whether the action is working correctly and what is the impact of the event on your environment. The following screenshot is an example:

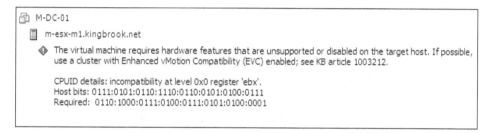

Note that the preceding screenshot contains several steps to find and fix problems in your environment, and in some cases it might take some time to go through all the steps. You should make a quick assessment of the discovered event and determine quickly how severe it is. If this discovery is going to cause problems quickly or have a far-reaching impact, then you need to open a case with your support company (VMware or others) right away. In some cases, you might not have the time to go through a step-by-step workflow and need to get things fixed quickly. An experienced administrator should know when the problem needs immediate attention. After you contact the support team/company, you can start to dig into the issue using the method we outlined earlier.

Does the incident have a negative impact?

Start your troubleshooting by gathering information to develop a better understanding of the questionable incident, and also collect pertinent information about the environment in which the incident occurred. Understand the conditions that are present while the incident occurred. Is the issue specific to a host, network component, storage or some other specific area of the environment?

Have you used the feature/option before and are you familiar with its actions? If this is a new feature to you, is it working in a different way than you would expect? Were there changes to hardware, or updates to the vSphere software components?

Take your time and verify the problem. This could provide you with clues to the cause and show that the incident is not a problem after all. This can prevent the administrator from wasting their time and effort on a "false" problem caused by a misunderstanding of the issue. There is no reason to accept a report that something is wrong without taking the time to verify the supposed problem.

 The time invested by an administrator up front could save plenty of time further down the road.

There could be times when an apparent error might not be a real error after all.

- The message might make it appear to be an error when it's actually a warning

- The design of the event could make it seem like an error, especially if the results are not what the administrator expects

Therefore, your best first step in troubleshooting is to verify that you really do have a problem. If available, you should click the context-sensitive Help buttons, wizards or reference to additional information (Knowledge Base articles) as shown in the following screenshot:

This could help to determine whether the message just a warning, or whether the questionable incident is a feature running the way that it should. If you find the incident is really not a problem, take some time to document what you have found to prevent spending time on it if it occurs again. Keeping good records of events in your environment is always time well spent, not only for you, but also for anyone that could assume responsibility for the environment in the future. After the issue is documented, consider the item to be closed.

If you find that the incident is truly a problem, there is a good chance it will have a negative impact on the environment. If not now, then at some point in the future. At this point, you should have all the information collected regarding the incident along with all the current conditions mentioned earlier. Now you need to try and understand the incident to predict its impact on your environment.

Understand the incident to document the impact

The dilemma you are faced with at this point is how much can you learn about the incident without negatively impacting your production environment. The more information you can gather and document on the problem will help put a priority on the resolution or how quickly you should submit it to technical support team. This will also allow you to explain why the issue needs to be addressed now or why it can wait until later. If there is a possibility of lost data or a larger outage, you need the information to be available to those who need to know. At this point, the evaluation of the incident relies on your knowledge of the environment. It is quite possible that the issue presents a low risk of negative impact and you have time to schedule downtime for correction. Again, knowing your environment, the tolerance for loss of information, and a close monitoring of your systems while the problem exists, will all need to be considered.

Most problems have occurred before and, if you have the time, researching solution tools such as Knowledge Bases can help you understand the problem along with the possible impact. The more you know about what you are facing, the better decision you will make about how and when to attack the problem. Also, research will allow you to determine if you can fix this on your own or need to open a support request.

Is it possible to isolate the incident?

After you determine that there is a real problem, the next thing to do is try to isolate the problem by reducing the factors that could be causing it. You want to eliminate items, one by one, that could be contributing to the unwanted results until you have a minimum number of factors but are still seeing the error. Do not change too many variables at once. You can see the behavior stop and will not know which factor was causing the problem. So you need to determine whether you can isolate the problem or not.

Remove unrelated variables

For instance, if your problem occurs with the vSphere cluster, is it possible to try the same thing on a single host? This will eliminate several factors that are associated with the cluster. If the problem does not occur, then that could point to a problem within the cluster or cluster configuration. If the problem is still happening when you connect to the host only, again try to eliminate additional items to narrow the number of variables involved.

The following screenshot shows that the incident occurs when migrating the virtual machine from one cluster to the other:

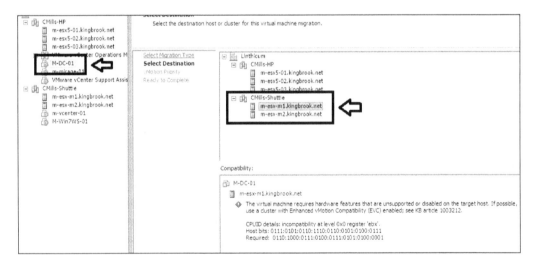

The incident is not seen when migrating the virtual machine to a host in the same cluster. This allows focus on the other cluster or the hosts within the cluster to determine what is causing the issue.

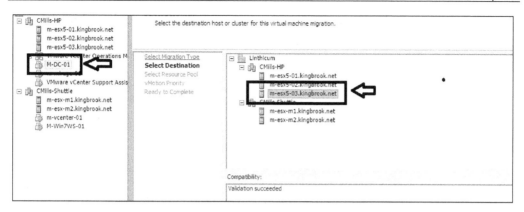

The other areas that you should look to narrow you variables would be:

- Networking
- Storage
- Virtual machines
- Physical host (moving the VM to another host)
- Physical host equipment
- Time configurations
- Active Directory – DNS settings

While you use the elimination process, be sure to document what you have done. This will help if there are many factors and you don't want to lose your place in the process. The information you collect can be used if you decide to submit a request. Also, this can help in reproducing the incident as discussed in the upcoming section. All this will educate you on your environment and can be useful in the future.

After you have taken the time to eliminate variables and have got to the point that you still have the problem and the information documented, you should verify your work and move to the next step of repeating the incident.

Are you able to repeat the incident?

Determine that you are able to reproduce the error after you have removed variables and recorded what you have done. This process might happen several times while different variables are being tested.

The following screenshot shows the incident with one of the virtual machines:

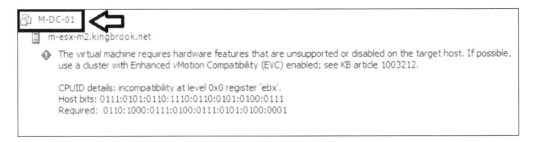

The following screenshot shows that the error can be repeated with another virtual machine:

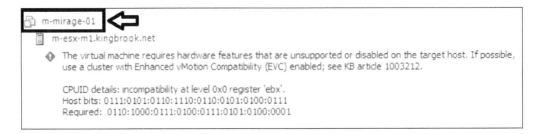

Attempt to reproduce and record variables

Use all the information you have collected about the unwanted incident, and as mentioned several times, document the information collected. At this point, you are running through your different options and you records are informal. After you have completed the testing and feel confident about reproducing the incident, move to the next section.

The following screenshot shows the select VM and the resulting incident when you attempt to migrate to another host found in the other cluster:

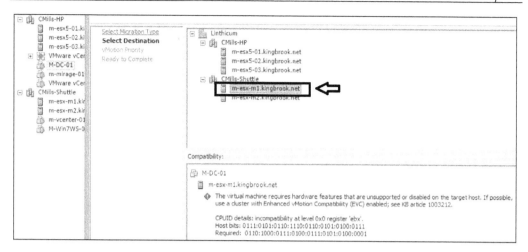

The following screenshot shows the same VM and a migration attempt to a host in a different cluster:

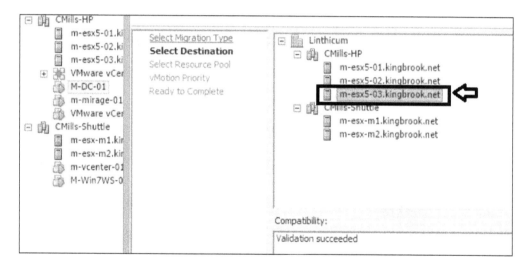

Now, the following screenshot shows the same incident on a different host in the other cluster. This shows that the incident can be reproduced, yet there are variables that can produce a different result, as discovered in the second screenshot we saw earlier.

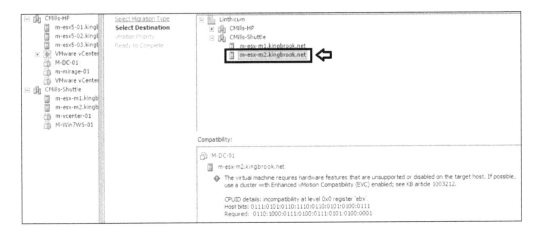

Your attempt in this process is to prove that the incident can be repeated, but there are factors that can change the outcome.

Record relevant information

This should be the formal record of your work. The recorded information helps you in understanding your environment, provides information if you need to submit the problem, and allows others to solve the same problem faster, if it happens again.

Can the cause be found and corrected?

You have spent a great deal of time investigating the questionable event that has invaded your environment. You have researched the issue to make sure it's not just a feature or function that you do not understand. You have read to make sure it's not a new feature or an option you never used before. You made sure to check whether it is an issue around a poorly named feature that has a misleading label. After you determined it was a problem, you started to eliminate variables to try and narrow down the cause. You spent time documenting your options to be sure you explored all the possible scenarios. Now that we have completed all of that, there are two more questions, "Do I know and understand the cause?" and "Can I fix this myself?". The answer to this decision box will decide your next step.

Submitting the problem to the customer support team

If the answer is no to both of the questions in the preceding section, then you need to open a support ticket with your vendor. All the work you did to research this problem and all the documentation you produced will be extremely helpful when you submit the problem. You will follow the process developed by the vendor to open a case with them. You should have an option to include additional information with the submission. If not, hold on to your valuable information until the vendor contacts you. The process will be different for each vendor, but each should provide a method for tracking the status of your problem.

Close and document

If you have answered yes to the question regarding cause and fixing, then you need to plan your next steps. You should complete the fix according to the business processes of your company. The process should not be disruptive and might need to be scheduled during nonproduction time.

The following information should be used as a guide only as it may not fit your business process. Here are some things to consider:

- Have a plan to fix the problem.
- Make sure you can prove that the problem is resolved.
- Plan testing to make sure you don't create a new problem by fixing the original one.
- Have a rollback plan, if possible.
- Continue to document your process as you go through your plan. The original plan might not work or requires modifications.
- Have a consultant or some other method of support on call.
- Give yourself enough time to complete the work without being rushed.
- Allow time for testing.

After all is completed, make sure your documentation is up to date and monitor your environment to make sure there are no other problems. While these type of issues are what administrators worry about, it is a great opportunity to learn about your environment. Spending the time to research and document will pay off in the long run.

Summary

This chapter provides information on an approach you can use when you discover an incident in your environment that produces results you did not expect. The purpose of this chapter is to provide a troubleshooting workflow that anyone can adapt for their environment. Collecting information, testing, and documenting your steps will help you with the following:

- To determine whether the incident is normal and whether any further action is needed

- To help determine that it is a problem and then find the cause, create a plan, and correct the problem

- To determine that there is a problem and a support ticket should be opened along with all the documented information available to assist in the resolution

Trouble in the environment is going to happen and it's important to quickly understand the impact and make decisions to begin the resolution process. This chapter gives you a framework to develop problem solving workflow. Use the information in this chapter and modify it to your business process, to help fix problems and keep you vSphere healthy.

Index

A

Active Directory (AD)
about 37
authentication, in vCenter SSO 5.5 47-49
administrator password
resetting, with VCSA 5.1 41
resetting, with VCSA 5.6 43
all-paths-down (APD) 89

B

backup
creating, of VMware Directory Service
database 123, 124
creating, of Windows registry keys 122, 123
backup, on Inventory Service database for
Windows
reference link 2
best practices, for upgrading vCenter to
vSphere 6
about 1
basic compatibility, verifying 2
database, preparing before upgrade 2
network prerequisites, verifying before
upgrade 3, 4
ODBC communication with database,
verifying 5
time synchronization, across vSphere
environment 5

C

CD-ROM Drive
vCenter Server Appliance (VCSA),
updating from 46
command line
used, for unmounting LUN 91-93
credential
adding, to Management Pack 100

D

data scrubbing option 142
datastores detaching
automating, with PowerCLI 93
disk I/O performance
ESXi host and VM disk I/O information,
obtaining 56
increasing 65
information, obtaining with Service Console
ESXi Shell 59-61
information, obtaining with vSphere
client 57-59
overview 55, 56
Distributed Resource Scheduler (DRS) 85
domain controller (DC) 4

E

End User License Agreement (EULA) 98

Thank you for buying
vCenter Troubleshooting

About Packt Publishing

Packt, pronounced 'packed', published its first book, *Mastering phpMyAdmin for Effective MySQL Management*, in April 2004, and subsequently continued to specialize in publishing highly focused books on specific technologies and solutions.

Our books and publications share the experiences of your fellow IT professionals in adapting and customizing today's systems, applications, and frameworks. Our solution-based books give you the knowledge and power to customize the software and technologies you're using to get the job done. Packt books are more specific and less general than the IT books you have seen in the past. Our unique business model allows us to bring you more focused information, giving you more of what you need to know, and less of what you don't.

Packt is a modern yet unique publishing company that focuses on producing quality, cutting-edge books for communities of developers, administrators, and newbies alike. For more information, please visit our website at www.packtpub.com.

About Packt Enterprise

In 2010, Packt launched two new brands, Packt Enterprise and Packt Open Source, in order to continue its focus on specialization. This book is part of the Packt Enterprise brand, home to books published on enterprise software – software created by major vendors, including (but not limited to) IBM, Microsoft, and Oracle, often for use in other corporations. Its titles will offer information relevant to a range of users of this software, including administrators, developers, architects, and end users.

Writing for Packt

We welcome all inquiries from people who are interested in authoring. Book proposals should be sent to author@packtpub.com. If your book idea is still at an early stage and you would like to discuss it first before writing a formal book proposal, then please contact us; one of our commissioning editors will get in touch with you.

We're not just looking for published authors; if you have strong technical skills but no writing experience, our experienced editors can help you develop a writing career, or simply get some additional reward for your expertise.

Disaster Recovery using VMware vSphere Replication and vCenter Site Recovery Manager

ISBN: 978-1-78217-644-2   Paperback: 162 pages

Learn to deploy and use vSphere Replication 5.5 as a standalone disaster recovery solution and to orchestrate disaster recovery using vCenter Site Recovery Manager 5.5

1. Learn how to deploy and use vSphere Replication as a standalone disaster recovery solution.

2. Configure SRM to leverage array-based or vSphere replication engine.

VMware vCenter Operations Manager Essentials

ISBN: 978-1-78217-696-1   Paperback: 246 pages

Explore virtualization fundamentals and real-world solutions for the modern network administrator

1. Written by VMware expert Lauren Malhoit, this book takes a look at vCenter Operations Manager from a practical point of view that every administrator can appreciate.

2. Understand, troubleshoot, and design your virtual environment in a better and more efficient way than you ever have before.

Please check **www.PacktPub.com** for information on our titles

VMware vSphere Resource Management Essentials

ISBN: 978-1-78217-046-4   Paperback: 112 pages

Optimum solutions to help you manage your VMware vSphere resources effectively

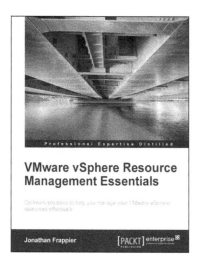

VMware vSphere Resource Management Essentials

Optimum solutions to help you manage your VMware vSphere resources effectively

Jonathan Frappier

1. Understand the requirements to build a strong virtual foundation and the features that can support your VMware environment.

2. Monitor and automate the tools available to make your VMware vSphere environment more efficient.

3. Packed with practical methods and techniques that will enhance your resource management in VMware.

VMware vSphere 5.x Datacenter Design Cookbook

ISBN: 978-1-78217-700-5   Paperback: 260 pages

Over 70 recipes to design a virtual datacenter for performance, availability, manageability, and recoverability with VMware vSphere 5.x

VMware vSphere 5.x Datacenter Design Cookbook

Over 70 recipes to design a virtual datacenter for performance, availability, manageability, and recoverability with VMware vSphere 5.x

Hersey Cartwright

1. Innovative recipes, offering numerous practical solutions when designing virtualized datacenters.

2. Identify the design factors — requirements, assumptions, constraints, and risks — by conducting stakeholder interviews and performing technical assessments.

Please check **www.PacktPub.com** for information on our titles

www.ingramcontent.com/pod-product-compliance
Lightning Source LLC
Chambersburg PA
CBHW060134060326
40690CB00018B/3868